CHRONOLOGY AND DOCUMENTARY
HANDBOOK OF THE
STATE OF
ALASKA

ELLEN LLOYD TROVER,

State Editor

WILLIAM F. SWINDLER,

Series Editor

1972 OCEANA PUBLICATIONS, INC./ Dobbs Ferry, New York

This is Volume 2 in the series CHRONOLOGIES AND DOCUMENTAR
HANDBOOKS OF THE STATES.

HOUSTON PUBLIC LIBRARY

© Copyright 1972 by Oceana Publications, Inc.

Library of Congress Cataloging in Publication Data
Main entry under title:

Chronology and documentary handbook of the State of
  Alaska.

  (Chronologies and documentary handbooks of the
States, v 2)
  SUMMARY: Contains a chronology of historical events
in Alaska, a biographical directory, an outline of the
state constitution and selected documents pertinent to
Alaskan history.
  Bibliography: p.
  1. Alaska--History--Chronology. 2. Alaska--
History--Sources. [1. Alaska--History]
I. Trover, Ellen Lloyd, ed. II Series.
F904.C45   979.8   72-2484
ISBN 0-379-16127-3

Manufactured in the United States of America

CONTENTS

CONTENTS

INTRODUCTION

This projected series of *Chronologies and Documentary Handbooks of the States* will ultimately comprise fifty separate volumes – one for each of the states of the Union. Each volume is intended to provide a concise ready reference of basic data on the state, and to serve as a starting point for more extended study as the individual user may require. Hopefully, it will be a guidebook for a better informed citizenry – students, civic and service organizations, professional and business personnel, and others.

The editorial plan for the *Handbook* series falls into five divisions: (1) a chronology of selected events in the history of the state; (2) a short biographical directory of the principal public officials, e.g., governors, Senators and Representatives; (3) an analytical outline of the state constitution; (4) the text of some representative documents illustrating main currents in the political, economic, social or cultural history of the state; and (5) a selected bibliography for those seeking further or more detailed information. Most of the data found in the present volume, in fact, have been taken from one or another of these references.

The user of these *Handbooks* may ask why the full text of the state constitution, or the text of constitutional documents which affected the history of the state, have not been included. There are several reasons: In the case of the current constitution, the text in almost all cases is readily available from one or more official agencies within the state. In addition, the current constitutions of all fifty states, as well as the federal Constitution, are regularly kept up to date in the definitive collection maintained by the Legislative Drafting Research Fund of Columbia University and published by the publisher of the present series of *Handbooks*. These texts are available in most major libraries under the title, *Constitutions of the United States: National and State*, in two volumes, with a companion volume, the *Index Digest of State Constitutions*.

Finally, the complete collection of documents illustrative of the constitutional development of each state, from colonial or territorial status up to the current constitution as found in the Columbia University collection, is being prepared for publication in a multi-volume series by the present series editor. Whereas the present series of *Handbooks* is intended for a wide range of interested citizens, the series of annotated constitutional materials in the volumes of *Sources and Documents of U.S. Constitutions* is primarily for the specialist in government, history or law. This is not to suggest that the general citizenry may not profit equally from referring to these materials; rather, it points up the separate purpose of the *Handbooks*, which is to guide the user to these and other sources of authoritative information with which he may systematically enrich his knowledge of this state and its place in the American Union.

William F. Swindler
Series Editor

vi

CHRONOLOGY

1728-1970

CHRONOLOGY

1728   *August 8.* Vitus Bering, Danish-born sea captain in service of Imperial Russia, sailed from Kamchatka in Siberia to determine whether Asia and North America were connected by land or separated by sea. He discovered entrance to present Bering Strait.

1731   A Cossack commander, Gwosdef, sailing to subjugate natives in easternmost Siberia, was blown onto Alaskan mainland near Norton Sound.

1741   *July 15.* Bering's second expedition of exploration sighted southern coast of Alaskan mainland. One of ships, the *St. Paul*, logged discovery of coast near Cape Muzon.

   July 16. Another of Bering's ships, the *St. Peter*, discovered coast near Mount St. Elias. After cursory observations, expedition wandered through Aleutian Islands, where Bering died.

1743   Attracted by indications of great fur resources, an expedition under Emil Bassof and other *promyshleniki* (traders) began voyages to the Aleutians.

1749   Ministers of Empress Elizabeth established a system of collecting tribute from Aleutians in form of furs. This imperial revenue service was placed under one Nevodchikof, who held the title of master of the imperial navy.

1764   Under orders from Catherine the Great, a Lieutenant Synd undertook a four-year exploration of the mainland of Alaska, and landed near the present site of Nome.

1772   The governor-general of Siberia transferred the administration of the Aleutian Islands to the commander of the post at Bolsheretsk in Kamchatka.

1

1774   The Spanish viceroy in Mexico, concerned at the
            news of expanding settlements in "Russian America,"
            ordered a series of expeditions to extend northward
            the Spanish claims to the western coast.

1775   Spanish and Russian explorations now began to
            overlap, with an expedition under Lt. Juan Francisco
            Quada in the ship *Sonora* sailing to the vicinity of
            Sitka. Meantime, Russian southward explorations
            would eventually provide a basis for claims as far as
            northern California.

1778   *May*. English rivalry in this area began with Captain
            James Cook's systematic survey of the coastline from
            Sitka through the Bering Strait to the Arctic Circle,
            an exploit which also finally confirmed the existence
            of a water corridor between Siberia and North
            America.

1781   Group of eastern Siberian merchants organized fur
            trading company under Gregory Shelekhov to
            develop regular market for exchange with Aleutian
            and Alaskan tribes.

1783   *August 16*. Three ships under Shelekhov sailed with
            192 men to establish first permanent Russian
            settlement in Alaska, near present-day Kodiak.
            Imperial government acquiesced in project since it
            consolidated Russian claims in face of Spanish and
            English rivalries in this area.

1785   Broadening base of settlement at Kodiak was
            exemplified in the establishment of a school in the
            colony.

            Russian imperial interest in the area was further
            demonstrated by edict of Catherine the Great,
            appointing Joseph Billings, a veteran of Captain
            Cook's expeditions, to command "A Secret
            Astronomical and Geographical Expedition for
            Navigating the Frozen Ocean."

1786   *June 12*. The Pribilof or Seal Islands were discovered by Gerassim Pribilof, son of a veteran of the Bering expeditions.

1788   Pressure from Spanish expeditions and British fur trading companies led to Russian edict giving Shelekhov company exclusive jurisdiction over all territory to which its discoveries extended. Two Spanish envoys, Estevan Martinez and Gonzales Hara, visited Russian officials at Kodiak.

1790   Martin Sauer of the Billings expedition wrote detailed description of Kodiak and adjacent areas, one of a series of published works which broadened European awareness of this part of North America.

1793   British establishment in western Canada was consolidated by the complete charts and maps prepared by George Vancouver, one of Captain Cook's veterans, relating to most of southeastern Alaska. At same time Alexander Mackenzie of Northwest Fur Company completed overland expedition to the coast.

1799   After a decade of destructive rivalries between Shelekhov company and other Siberian groups, as well as with English fur trading companies, Czar Paul granted charter to a new agency, the Russian-America Company, under 20-year renewable terms. This agency was to become the quasi-governmental organization for the remainder of the Russian tenure in Alaska.

1802   English challenge to Russian jurisdiction took form of trading post established near Sitka, one of points where overland and coastal activities of Canadian fur trade were expected to meet.

1811   Russian authorities ousted English settlers near Sitka, as part of systematic expansion of Russian settlements down coast and inland.

1818   *January 11*. Captain Leontii Andreevich Hagemeister
                       of the Russian navy became chief manager of
                       Russian-American Company. He succeeded Alexander
                       Andreevich Baranov, who had served for 28 years as
                       manager and governor. Hagemeister had participated
                       in earlier attempts of Shelekhov company to
                       establish trading posts in Hawaii.

                       October 24. Semen Ivanovich Yanovski, son-in-law of
                       Baranov and assistant to Hagemeister, succeeded
                       Hagemeister as chief manager. He made extensive
                       surveys of coastal waters of area, filling in many
                       details on earlier explorers' maps.

1820   *September 15*. Mihael Ivanovich Muraviev became
                       manager-governor. He had long experience in the
                       company and had effected a number of reforms
                       which it was anticipated would become permanent if
                       the company charter was to be renewed.

1821   *September 4*. Attempting to discourage ships of other
                       nations from trading with Alaskan posts, an imperial
                       edict proclaimed 100-mile limit on territorial waters
                       in this area.

                       September 21. Charter of Russian-American
                       Company was renewed for second 20-year term.
                       Extensive revisions of original charter brought
                       company under greater government control and
                       sought to redress many grievances of settlers caused
                       by arbitrary rule of company officials in past.

1824   *April 5*. Treaty signed between United States and
                       Russia relaxed edict of previous year by permitting
                       free trade in Alaskan ports by American ships, for
                       ten-year period. Treaty recognized the 54 degrees 40
                       minutes northern limit which U.S. was seeking to
                       establish as its border with Canada.

                       October 14. Peter Egorovich Chistiakov became chief
                       manager of Russian American Company. He reopened

1824   port of Sitka to foreign ships and negotiated many of the details for settlement of border dispute with Canada, covered by treaty the following year.

1825   *February*. Britain and Russia signed free trade treaty with reference to Alaska, and agreed upon a crudely surveyed border line between territories of both nations in this area. Greatest gain for Britain was right of navigation to sea, through Russian territory, for boats of Hudson's Bay Company traveling on streams which originated in Canada.

1830   *June 1*. Baron Friedrich Petrovich von Wrangell became manager-governor. Wrangell was the best known Arctic explorer of his day, and his intimate knowledge of Alaska made him Czars' advisor on subject for remainder of Russian era in Alaska.

1832   First discovery of gold in Alaska, near Kuskokwim River.

1835   *October 29*. Ivan Antonovich Kupreanof became manager-governor. With severe smallpox outbreak among coastal settlements, he urged attempts at new inland settlements.

1840   *May 25*. Adolf Karlovich Etolin became manager-governor. Reportedly born in Sitka, Etolin was a longtime resident of the area and devoted next twenty years to urging improved educational and other public services for region.

1841   *March 5*. A third charter for Russian American Company was agreed upon in principle, although three years would be spent in working out details of renewal. Part of delay was caused by change in imperial policy, emphasizing trade with China as complement to established fur trade in northern Pacific.

1841   As part of this reorientation of imperial policy,
            Russian Fort Ross in California was sold to John
            Sutter and Russian settlers evacuated to Alaska.

1844   *October 10.* Czar Nicholas I officially approved new
            charter of company. Changes in charter gave
            government greater control over administrative
            affairs. Czar's ministers urged greater attention to
            promoting settlements; after a century of territorial
            control, native Russians in Alaska numbered only 633
            persons.

1845   *July 9.* Michael Dmitrievitch Tebenkof became
            manager-governor. Under von Wrangell, Tebenkof had
            conducted extensive exploration of Yukon area and
            undertook a series of plans - none too successful - to
            encourage greater pace of immigration from Russia.

1847   British pressure on Alaska increased with
            establishment of Fort Yukon by Hudson's Bay
            Company in defiance of Russian jurisdiction. Primary
            threat to Russian interest was prospect that Canadian
            traders could attract natives from coastal areas to
            barter for goods brought over inland waterways to
            Yukon.

1848   First whaler, the American ship *Superior*, sailed
            through Bering Strait, offering new type of economic
            competition for Russians.

1850   *October 14.* Nikolai Yakovlevich Rosenberg became
            manager-governor.

1852   New market for Russians opened with visit of
            American ship *Bacchus*, seeking purchase of cargoes
            of ice for sale in San Francisco. This led to formation
            of "Ice Company," later a political force in Alaskan
            purchase.

1853   *March 31.* Alexander Ilich Rudakof became
            manager-governor.

1854   *April 22.* Stephen Vasilii Voevodski became
                manager-governor. The rapid decline of the fur trade,
                both because of overkill of the animals and the
                collapse of China market, together with invasion of
                Alaskan waters by American whalers, depressed
                company prospects and encouraged initial interest in
                selling territory.

1856   Senator William Gwin of California introduced bill to
                purchase Alaska for $5,000,000. Rumors of gold in
                the territory, and general spirit of expansionism in
                this period, aroused western interest in proposal.
                Russia had made tentative offer during Crimean War,
                and James Buchanan before becoming President had
                also considered the possibility of purchase.

                June 22. Ivan V. Furuhelm became
                manager-governor. A Finnish mining engineer,
                Furuhelm's appointment suggested an effort on the
                part of the company and the government to explore
                the potential resources of the territory now that the
                fur trade was in decline and sporadic discoveries of
                gold were being reported.

1857   First sizable gold discovery on Fraser River
                stimulated rush of settlers to region, but these were
                almost all from Canada and United States. Gold talk
                revived California interest in acquiring territory for
                United States.

1861   Serious discussion of possible sale of Alaska began in
                Russia, ardently advocated by Baron Edouard de
                Stoeckl because of prospect that Britain would renew
                war against Russia and seize all of Russian America.
                Outbreak of Civil War in United States suspended
                these discussions.

1863   Russian government failed to issue new charter to
                Russian American Company, despite vigorous
                protests of stockholders and advocates of continued

1863   colonial policy. Rumors of effort to sell territory undermined company's credit; conversely, failure of charter renewal meant assumption of all administrative expense of territory by imperial government.

December 2. Prince Dmitri Maksoutoff became last Russian governor, although government vacillation on proposal of sale left future of territory in doubt.

1866   Legislature of Washington territory petitioned Congress to seek new fishing concessions off Alaskan coast.

December 16. After prolonged debate in Czar's government, it was decided to invite firm offer of purchase from United States, and Baron de Stoeckl was empowered to open negotiations.

1867   *March 29.* Stoeckl formally advised Secretary of State William H. Seward that Russia would accept offer of $7,200,000. The two men worked all night on draft of treaty of purchase, which was signed by them the next day.

April 9. After vigorous debate, Senate reluctantly brought ratification to vote, barely winning necessary two-thirds majority, 27-12. On resubmission of question seeking formal record of unanimity, two Senators continued to hold out, and final official vote was 37-2.

June 20. Ratification of treaty formally proclaimed.

1868   Congress engaged in prolonged debate over appropriation of funds for purchase of Alaska. Aside from western representatives, American public generally agreed that territory was of little value and termed it "Seward's Folly." General lack of enthusiasm over sale in Russia was almost equal to that in United States.

1868   *September 19.* Anticipating general influx of settlers from the United States, Barney O'Regan established first newspaper, the Sitka *Times.* This paper succeeded the *Alaska Times*, established previous spring.

October 18. General Lovell H. Rousseau of U.S. Army formally received transfer of Alaska from Russian Captain Aleksei Pestchouroff at Sitka. General William H. Davis made pessimistic preliminary report that widespread Indian hostility would require systematic military establishment before general settlement by American immigrants would be feasible.

Congress extended customs laws of United States to new territory, placed Pribilof Islands under supervision of Secretary of Treasury, and directed that criminal jurisdiction of territory be vested in Federal courts of Washington, Oregon and California.

1869   *August 2.* New city council of Sitka, concerned at apparent plan of Congress to leave Alaska indefinitely under military administration as result of Davis report, urged Secretary of State Seward, then visiting territory, to seek establishment of civil government.

1870   No attempt was made by United States to take census of new territory, but incomplete unofficial estimates were less than 31,000 persons, of whom about 500 were Russians about to leave and 300 were Americans. Brief influx of fortune-seekers had overbuilt townsites which now were derelicts.

Alaska Commercial Company, first American enterprise of significance, received 20-year lease on Pribilof Islands. Company formed permanent lobby in Washington to discourage civil government in territory.

1872   *December 2.* In his message to Congress, President
             Grant offered no program of development of Alaska
             as territory but called attention to need for a border
             commission to clarify boundary between Alaska and
             Canada.

1873   The Sitka city council, only semblance of civil
             government in territory, dissolved because of lack of
             interest and lack of legal authority to raise funds.

             Congress amended customs laws to forbid sale of
             liquor to Indians in territory.

1874   Henry W. Elliott, special agent of Treasury
             Department, published critical report of territorial
             conditions and recommending some form of civil
             government. He concluded that population would
             never be large enough to justify fullscale territorial
             status. His conclusions were disputed by Major W. G.
             Morris, his successor as agent in the seal island
             territories.

1875   General Howard, commanding officer of the military
             forces in territory, urged Congress to create a civil
             government with judicial powers over widespread
             crime, stating that he lacked either authority or
             organization to administer police service.

1877   *June 14.* Disinterested in this distant possession,
             Congress not only ignored recommendations for
             organizing civil administration but began withdrawing
             troops for other areas. By this date the last army
             forces departed, and Alaska had no United States
             official in residence except the customs officer at
             Sitka.

1878   Miss Fannie Kellogg and John G. Brady (later
             governor) founded Presbyterian mission school at
             Sitka.

1879   Indian depredations, provoked by absence of armed
                forces in territory, terrorized Sitka and other
                struggling outposts of area. Residents petitioned
                Congress for protection, and eventually a naval vessel,
                the *Jamestown*, was dispatched to Sitka as token of
                protection.

                July 1. Captain L. A. Beardslee of the *Jamestown*
                called a town meeting to seek to interest residents in
                Sitka in reviving town council. Elections were held in
                October, but before end of year council had become
                moribund for lack of interest.

1880   Federal census officials still did not attempt to count
                population in territory; unofficial estimate was
                33,426, mostly Indian.

1881   *July*. Col. M. D. Ball, customs collector at Sitka, was
                elected as delegate to Congress, but not seated
                because territory had not been authorized to form
                government or elect such a delegate. Incident called
                public attention to critical need for Congressional
                action on territory.

                December. Joseph Juneau, a French Canadian, made
                first major gold strike in area north of Sitka. With
                rush of goldseekers and miners, military law was
                imposed in effort to control widespread violence.
                New town of Juneau, near site of gold strike, in two
                years had population of more than 1,000 persons.

1884   *May 17*. Congress finally adopted statute for
                organization of a civil government for Alaska
                Territory. Laws of Oregon were extended to Alaska
                and a district court established to hold at least two
                terms annually.

                July 4. President Arthur appointed J.H. Kinkead,
                former territorial governor of Nevada and a merchant
                in Sitka since 1867, as first governor of Territory of
                Alaska.

1884

September 15. With formal establishment of civil government under the organic act of May 17, naval jurisdiction over nonmilitary personnel in territory was terminated.

1885

May 7. President Cleveland appointed Alfred P. Swineford of Michigan as territorial governor. Swineford, an ex-newspaperman and supporter of local rule for Alaska, strongly criticized fishing and canning companies which opposed greater administrative power in local agencies as threat to their monopolies.

President Cleveland requested congressional appropriation of $100,000 to make preliminary reconnoiter of Alaskan-Canadian border. This question, which had become acute after organization of Canada into confederation in 1871, grew out of inaccuracies in original maps on which Russian-English border agreement had been based. Congress, disinterested in this remote area, failed to make the appropriation.

1886

Bering Sea fisheries dispute between United States, Russia and Great Britain reached critical stage when American authorities announced a closed season on taking of seals on high seas. U.S. revenue cutter *Corwin* took three Canadian sealers into custody and precipitated international crisis.

1887

Bering Sea crisis mounted with seizure of six American and six Canadian sealers by revenue cutter *Richard Rush.* British foreign office alerted its fleet units in northern Pacific to prepare to resist American efforts to arrest other sealers in this area. British insisted American jurisdiction extended only to three-mile limit and did not include international waters.

1889   *March 2.* Congress enacted law directing President to
             issue annual warning to other nations against pelagic
             (high sea) sealing, with particular reference to Bering
             Sea. American position was that closed season on seals
             ashore was ineffective unless extended into
             international waters. Powerful fisheries and canning
             lobbies in Washington worked to undermine
             American efforts toward an international settlement.

             April 20. President Harrison appointed Lyman E.
             Knapp, a Civil War veteran and native of Vermont, as
             territorial governor. Knapp felt two strongest needs
             of Alaska to be organization of municipal government
             and delegate in Congress.

1890   Responding to Governor Knapp's proposal for local
             government, Congress enacted statute providing for
             incorporation of towns and local school boards.
             Territorial organization in Alaska was still
             rudimentary, and delegate question was not to be
             settled for fifteen more years.

             The first systematic census indicated total population
             of 32,052 persons.

             March. State Department rejected British proposal for
             arbitration of Bering Sea question, apparently as
             result of lobbying by west coast and Alaskan canning
             interests.

             June 14. British government filed solemn protest over
             continued American insistence on closed season on
             pelagic sealing, and again prepared to dispatch naval
             units to protect its shipping.

1891   Bering Sea crisis continued unsolved. Alaskan
             canneries opposed open sealing on high seas because
             this gave advantage to ships of other nations when
             fisheries licensed by United States were restricted to
             the time and number of seals they could take on land.

1892   *February*. American and Canadian representatives met in Washington to begin discussions of settlement of Alaskan boundary. Although settlement was still distant prospect, preliminary survey of coastal area, correcting old charts, was ordered.

        June 28. President Cleveland appointed James Sheakley, veteran of California gold rush, as territorial governor. Having lived in Alaska for six years, Sheakley was thus the first resident to be appointed to an official government office. He was also one of first Alaskan delegates to Democratic National Convention in 1891.

1896   Discovery of gold in Yukon district of Canada suddenly revived question of border settlement, as both American and Canadian customs agencies tried to regulate influx of gold seekers. Great numbers of adventurers precipitated crisis in peacekeeping agencies of territorial government.

1897   *June 4*. Congress authorized creation of commission to draft a revised criminal code for Alaska. Governor Sheakley had urged this as one of the most needed steps in strengthening of orderly government in territory, as gold rush continued to create problems of civil administration.

        June 16. John G. Brady became territorial governor. Having first come to Alaska as Presbyterian missionary, he had served as commissioner in land office at Sitka since 1884. He urged rapid conclusion of work on new criminal code, additional courts to administer law and delegate to Congress to make territory's needs known to nation.

        December 6. President McKinley in his annual message to Congress cautiously recommended more detailed organization of territorial government, including an appointed legislative council to frame local legislation.

1898   Joint U.S. - British commission sought to settle conflicts of both Alaskan-Canadian border and Atlantic and Bering Sea fisheries. Tentative settlement of fisheries policy was reached, but no satisfactory disposition of border question.

May 14. Congress extended homestead laws to Territory of Alaska, enlarging the claims to 80 acres and providing for railroad rights of way without review by the Interstate Commerce Commission, as means of enticing settlement and development of region.

1899   Prohibition laws for Alaska were repealed, partly due to impossibility of enforcement, and partly to promote revenues from liquor licenses.

March 3. New criminal code for territory was finally approved after more than two years of study by Congress. When this code went into effect, territory for first time had set of laws more nearly adapted to local conditions than laws of West Coast states which had been previously extended to it.

These statutory reforms by Congress increased demands of settlers for representation by delegate in Congress. Convention at Skagway called by chambers of commerce drew up proposals for additional legislation and elected its own delegate, John G. Price, who, however, was not seated on his arrival in Washington.

November. Governor Brady formally called for statehood for Alaska. This announcement was primarily for local political effect, since Washington was convinced that population was still too sparse even for fullscale territorial government. It did spur Congressional proposals for further statutory reforms, however.

1900   *June 6.* Carter Act, providing for comprehensive civil code for territory, rounded out a four-year program of Congressional provisions for Alaska but still left it without an elected legislature or delegate in Congress. Provision was made for removal of capital from Sitka to Juneau and for incorporation of all larger towns.

Governor Brady was appointed to another term.

Census figures showed 63,592 population.

1901   Although railroad construction languished, army engineers opened a pack trail from Valdez to the upper Yukon basin.

1902   *November.* J. W. Ivey, a former customs collector, was sent to Washington as another delegate from a local convention, seeking to persuade Congress to provide a seat for the territorial representative. Although this request was denied, Congress did receive his petition for revision of land laws, modification of liquor license provisions, and restriction on powers of attorney in locating missing claimants to mining property.

1903   *May.* President Theodore Roosevelt, on visit to Alaska, discussed with certain territorial representatives the problem of obtaining a delegate to Congress and promised his assistance on the matter.

Congress responded to Alaskan petitions by modifying homestead laws, enlarging claims to 320 acres and permitting settler to lay his own lines and file his papers on basis of his own survey.

United States and Great Britain signed a treaty, with reluctant acquiescence of Canada, to establish an arbitral tribunal of six jurists to settle Alaskan border question. American members of commission, visiting territory on U.S.S. *Dolphin*, found chief political concern of residents was delegate to Congress.

1903   *October 20.* Meeting in London, the boundary tribunal agreed on main features of Alaskan border advocated by United States.

1904   Governor Brady was reappointed to another term.

1905   Congress passed the Nelson Act, providing for a territorial organization of school districts for territory to be financed in part from licenses for business outside the towns which were paid into the "Alaska Fund." The governor was designated supervisor of public instruction.

January 27. The Alaska Road Commission was created by Congress. As subsequently revised, the statute provided for a body of Army engineers to develop plans for a transportation system in the territory.

April 10. The Supreme Court of the United States, in *Rasmussen v. United States* (197 U.S. 516), ruled that Alaska had been incorporated into the territory under the jurisdiction of the United States by the treaty of purchase.

November 18. In another flurry of activity to secure effective representation in Congress, a convention held in Seattle chose a three-man delegation to press the territory's case: ex-Governor Swineford was the chief advocate for stronger territorial government, but the other two members, Richard Tyan and O.J. Humphrey of Nome, represented the canning-fishing monopolies opposed to increased regulatory authority.

December 5. President Theodore Roosevelt formally recommended to Congress an official delegate to represent the territory.

1906   *March 2.* Wilfred B. Hogatt was appointed governor. He had come to Alaska in 1894 as a member of a

1906   hydrographic survey team and later acquired mining interests near Juneau. He was the first governor to make extensive visits to the interior and to the Seward Peninsula.

May 8. The Alaska Delegate Act, finally passed by Congress, was signed into law.

December 3. The first delegate, Frank H. Waskey of Nome, took his seat in Congress. A mining company executive, his election was largely honorary since it was only for the term ending the following March.

1907   *December 2.* The second delegate to take his seat was Thomas Cole of Fairbanks, a veteran mining operator.

The Alaskan Road Commission completed one of its first projects, widening the pack trail between Valdez and Fairbanks to make it passable for horse-drawn sleds in winter.

1908   The first significant railroad construction was a line financed by the Guggenheim-Morgan interests of New York, to open up a line to the copper fields near the Kennecott Glacier.

1909   Walter E. Clark of Connecticut was named territorial governor. Local newspapers condemned the appointment of a "carpetbagger," but President Taft had concluded that an outsider had the best chance of resolving a number of political conflicts which he believed were holding back the chances of self-government in the territory.

March 15. Judge James Wickersham of Fairbanks, a strong advocate of home rule and a vigorous critic of the Guggenheim mining empire, was elected the new territorial delegate.

A fourth judicial district was created for the territory. Since these districts performed many of the

1909   administrative functions ordinarily handled by counties, the creating of an additional district indicated growing need for local government organization.

December 7. Convinced that Alaska was not ready for a full-fledged territorial government, President Taft proposed that Congress create a commission form of government similar to that in the Philippines. Neither Congress nor Alaska approved the idea.

1910   The census indicated 64,356 population. This slow increase in inhabitants confirmed the official view in Washington that the territory was not yet able to support a full local government. Alaskans, however, insisted that home rule was their only hope of converting the territory into something besides a "prize package" for exploiting corporations.

1911   *April 4.* Judge Wickersham was seated for second term as delegate. On this date he introduced a bill to create a territorial legislature. Three weeks later a similar bill was introduced in the Senate.

July 7. The long dispute over pelagic sealing was concluded with the signing of the North Pacific Seal Convention by all nations interested in deep sea fisheries in the Bering Sea area.

1912   *August 24.* The Alaska Home Rule Bill became effective. It created a territorial legislature consisting of a senate of eight persons and a lower house of sixteen. On this same date, Congress adopted an act providing for a presidential commission to plan for construction of a railroad from the coast to the interior of the territory.

1913   The first automobile crossed the Richardson Trail from Valdez to Fairbanks.

1913   *April 7.* Judge Wickersham began his third term as delegate.

April 18. Major John F.A. Strong, a veteran newspaperman of the territory, was elected governor of the reorganized territorial political structure.

October 31. An abortive proposal was made in the House of Representatives, to trade the Alaska panhandle to Canada in return for British Honduras.

1914   The presidential commission on an Alaskan railroad reported on its findings to President Woodrow Wilson. The President recommended to Congress that an appropriation for construction be made, but with World War I and the difficulties involved in construction it was 1923 before the line was completed.

1915   *March 4.* Congress authorized the proceeds from the sale of certain sections of township sites to be set aside for construction of a territorial college and school of mines. A site near Fairbanks was set aside for the institution which became the University of Alaska.

Territorial legislature passed a liberal workmen's compensation law, reflecting consciousness of hazards in mining and fishing industries as well as generally progressive political outlook of legislature.

Further evidence of liberal nature of legislature was act enfranchising Indians and Eskimos. Washington administration challenged the legal right of the legislature to pass statute on the subject, and Congress itself did not confirm the action in a statute of enfranchisement until 1924.

December 6. Judge Wickersham returned to his seat in Congress for another term.

1916   *November.* A territorial referendum supported the reinstatement of prohibition in Alaska.

1917   *March 3.* Congress granted the territorial legislature power to take over and develop the territorial school system, outside of government schools maintained for natives.

         April 2. Charles A. Sulzer, an army veteran and miner, won the delegate's seat in Congress in a disputed election. Judge Wickersham successfully contested the seat the following January. Sulzer represented the growing strength of the Democratic party in what had long been a "safe" Republican area.

1918   *January 7.* Wickersham succeeded Sulzer in contested seat for delegate in Congress.

         April 12. Thomas Riggs, Jr. was appointed governor. He had been a member of the Alaska boundary survey and later a member of the commission supervising construction of the railway line.

1919   *April 15.* Charles A. Sulzer again won a disputed election for the delegate's seat, but died before the contest was decided.

         July 1. George B. Grigsby of Juneau was appointed to fill Sulzer's term and took his seat as delegate. Grigsby, an attorney, had been mayor of Nome in 1914.

1920   The territorial population was listed at 55,036.

         August 24. New York to Nome flight of four DeHaviland planes ushered in the air age to Alaska.

1921   *March 1.* Wickersham again was seated after successfully contesting seat won by Sulzer and held by Grigsby.

1921 *April 11*. The new territorial delegate was Daniel A. Sutherland, Canadian-born citizen of Massachusetts, who had served in the territorial legislature since 1912. He was active in fisheries and mining.

 June 16. S.C. Bone, former editor of the Seattle *Post-Intelligencer*, was appointed governor.

1922 *February 6*. Washington treaty on arms limitations forbade fortification of the Aleutians for fourteen years.

1923 *July 15*. President Warren G. Harding drove the ceremonial last spike to complete the Alaskan interior railway line.

 September 18. Territorial college, later the University of Alaska, was formally dedicated.

 October. City council of Juneau called for special election to vote on question of division of territory as preliminary to local government organization looking toward statehood.

 December 3. Sutherland reelected as territorial delegate.

1924 Congress belatedly ratified 1915 territorial act conferring franchise on Indians, Eskimos and Aleuts.

 Airmail service was inaugurated under Carl Ben Eielson, a commercial flyer under contract with the Post Office Department.

1925 *February*. Brigadier General William Mitchell, in testimony before Congressional committee, urged development of air defenses for Alaska.

 February 27. Glacier Bay National Monument was established by presidential proclamation.

1925   *June 13.* G.A. Parks, in charge of the Alaska Survey Office, was appointed territorial governor.

Abandoned army posts in territory were turned over to local government for use as training schools for natives.

December 7. Sutherland reelected as territorial delegate.

1927   *January.* President Coolidge replaced two district judges and U.S. Attorney for first judicial district, on ground that they had made no effort to stop bootlegging.

December 7. Sutherland reelected as delegate.

1929   *April 15.* Sutherland reelected as delegate.

September. Parks reappointed to second term as governor.

1930   Census showed population of 59,278 persons.

April. Official state flag for Alaska adopted.

1931   *December 7.* Judge Wickersham, longtime delegate to Congress, was reelected after a decade of private practice and extensive writing on Alaskan subjects.

1933   *March 9.* New territorial delegate was Anthony J. Dimond of Valdez, a miner and lawyer and veteran of territorial legislature.

April 19. John W. Troy of Juneau, editor of the *Daily Alaska Empire*, was appointed governor.

1934   *April 18.* The Secretary of War advised the House Committee on Highways that a highway to Alaska from the main part of the United States was feasible

1934   from an engineering viewpoint, but expressed no
            opinion as to its economic or military value.

1935   *January 3.* Delegate Dimond was reelected.

            February 4. President F.D. Roosevelt issued an
            executive order banning homesteading in the
            Matanuska Valley pending development of plans for a
            government-assisted colony.

            May 29. Lottery was held to assign tracts in
            Matanuska Valley for resettlement project intended
            as a depression relief measure. The Federal
            Emergency Relief Administration selected 200
            families for the colony.

1937   *January 5.* Dimond seated upon reelection as delegate.

            May. Governor Troy reappointed.

1938   The Alaskan International Highway Commission was
            created by President Roosevelt to develop plans for a
            highway through Canada to the territory. Military
            plans for Alaska, however, were so indefinite that
            Major General S.D. Butler urged abandonment of
            territory in case of war.

1939   *January 3.* Dimond reelected as seated as delegate.

            First military construction for defense in Alaska was
            in form of $4,000,000 appropriation for cold-weather
            experiment station at Fairbanks.

            Organized plan to campaign for statehood was
            announced by the Alaska Home Rule Association.
            The first step was to persuade Congress to vest full
            authority for territorial affairs in the legislature.

            December 5. Dr. Ernest H. Gruening of the
            Department of the Interior became territorial

1939   governor. Although a resident of Washington, D.C. Gruening quickly became an ardent student and writer on Alaskan affairs, and worked for eventual statehood.

1940   Population was reported as 72,524.

June. Small contingent of Army troops was sent to Anchorage to garrison Fort Richardson when its construction was completed. Governor Gruening began organization of a national guard to help in territorial defense.

August 18. United States and Canada established a joint board for planning far northern defenses, and agreed that Alaska would be the first line of defense.

1941   *January 3*. Delegate Dimond reelected and took seat. On February 5, he introduced bill proposing immediate start on construction of Alaskan defense highway through Canada. Later in year, military authorities advised that sea lanes could not be kept open in event of war with Japan.

1942   Territorial legislature was enlarged by act of Congress, senate to sixteen and house to twenty-four members.

January 12. Delegate Dimond made major speech urging all-out effort to construct highway to Alaska. President Roosevelt four days later created a Cabinet committee to report on the steps necessary to undertake such construction.

February 2. Cabinet committee, meeting with representatives of War Department, recommended immediate action on highway. Two weeks later construction began on Alaska-Canadian highway.

June 3. Japanese air attacks on Dutch Harbor were followed by capture and occupation of Kiska and Attu.

1943   *January 6.* Delegate Dimond reelected and seated.

Alaska statehood bill introduced into Congress.

May 11. American forces recaptured Attu after month's campaign.

August 15. Joint American and Canadian forces recaptured Kiska and ended military activity in Alaskan theater.

1945   As end of World War II approached, Alaskans resumed campaigns for statehood. Territorial legislature created state department of agriculture and Alaska Housing Authority to promote further settlement in area.

January 3. Edward L. Bartlett, secretary of the territory from 1939 to 1942 and later secretary to Delegate Dimond, succeeded him as territorial representative.

Alaska statehood bill introduced into Congress.

Secretary of Interior Harold L. Ickes endorsed statehood.

1946   Territorial legislature passed first veterans' aid bill in country.

Local referendum held on sentiment for statehood; vote was 9,630 for and 6,822 against.

1947   *January 3.* Delegate Bartlett reelected and seated.

Statehood bill, to become a regular proposal in each session of Congress, reintroduced.

1949   *January 3.* Delegate Bartlett reelected and seated.

1949   Territorial legislature adopted elaborate state tax code, thus providing realistic economic base for future statehood status.

Governor Gruening continued as governor, amid public expressions of praise for his wartime services in territory.

1950   Census listed territorial population at 128,643. This was substantially above population total traditionally treated by Congress as sufficient to qualify for statehood.

1951   *January 3*. Delegate Bartlett reelected and Alaska statehood bill reintroduced.

June 18. Daily passenger service on Alaska Railroad began between Fairbanks and Anchorage, dramatizing steady economic development of territory.

1953   *January 3*. Delegate Bartlett reelected.

February 24. B. Frank Heintzleman appointed territorial governor. A member of the U.S. Forest Service in Juneau, he was nationally known as authority on forestry and conservation.

1955   *January 5*. Delegate Bartlett reelected and seated.

Constitutional convention for territory was requested by legislature, preparatory to final drive for statehood.

September 13. Fifty-five delegates were elected to constitutional convention.

November 9. Constitutional convention opened at University of Alaska. Keynote address by former governor Gruening was entitled, "Let Us End American Colonialism."

1956   *April 24.* Two Senators and a Representative were conditionally elected to Congress in the hope of early action on statehood. They were William A. Egan, Valdez, and Ex-Governor Gruening as "Senators", and Ralph J. Rivers of Fairbanks, "Representative." This psychological effort was based on so-called "Tennessee plan" to expedite statehood, used in 1796.

1957   *January 3.* Delegate Bartlett reelected for last term as territorial representative.

Governor Heintzleman retired. Secretary of Territory Hendrickson appointed to serve out remainder of term.

May. President Eisenhower appointed M.A. Stepovich as the last territorial governor.

1958   *January 3.* Statehood bill signed into law. Statute provided for formal election by residents on question of accepting statehood.

August 26. Alaska voted for statehood, 40,452 to 7,010. Governor Stepovich resigned and Secretary Hendrickson again was appointed to serve out his term.

November. William A. Egan, veteran legislator and president of constitutional convention, was elected first governor of new state.

1959   *January 7.* Delegate Bartlett became first United States Senator from Alaska, with term ending January 3, 1961. Ex-Governor Gruening was seated as the junior Senator, with term ending January 3, 1963. The first U.S. Representative was Ralph J. Rivers of Fairbanks, veteran miner, attorney and state legislator.

Alaska began its state government under a constitution widely acclaimed as modern and

1959   efficient. Constitution had been drafted after
                scholarly study of both test and practical operation
                of constitutions in numerous states.

1960   Population of new state was listed at 226,167.

1963   *January 9*. Senator Gruening began full term, having
                been reelected previous fall.

1964   *March 27*. Great earthquake destroyed large portions
                of Kodiak and Seward. Anchorage and other areas
                also reported widespread damage.

1966   Eight separate regional groups joined to form the
                Alaska Federation of Natives, and prepared to submit
                claims to 370,000 acres of land by right of aboriginal
                use and occupancy.

                November. Walter J. Hickel was elected governor.

1967   *January 5*. Howard W. Pollock, Anchorage, seated as
                new Representative.

1968   Widespread petroleum deposits discovered at Prudhoe
                Bay by American and Canadian oil companies.
                Trans-Alaska Pipeline System organized soon
                thereafter to begin laying line from Prudhoe Bay to
                Valdez for oil development.

1969   Governor Hickel appointed Secretary of Interior;
                succeeded by Keith H. Miller.

                January 3. Mike Gravel, Anchorage, succeeded
                Senator Gruening.

1970   Latest population: 303,137.

BIOGRAPHICAL DIRECTORY

MANAGERS OF THE RUSSIAN AMERICAN COMPANY

Alexander Andreevich Baranof (1790-1818)
Leontii Andreanovich Hagemeister (Jan.-Oct. 1818)
Semen Ivanovich Yanovski (1818-20)
Matxei I. Muravief (1820-25)
Peter Egorovich Chistiakov (1825-30)
Baron Ferdinand von Wrangell (1830-35)
Ivan Antonovich Kupreanof (1835-40)
Adolph Karlovich Etolin (1840-45)
Michael D. Tebenkof (1845-50)
Nikolai Y. Rosenberg (1850-53)
Alexander Ilich Rudakof (1853-54)
Stephen Vasili Voevodski (1854-59)
Ivan V. Furuhelm (1859-63)
Prince Dmitri Maksoutoff (1863-67)

BONE, Scott C.
  b. Feb. 15, 1860, Shelby County, Ind.
  d. Jan. 27, 1936, Santa Barbara, Calif.
  Governor of territory, 1921-25

BRADY, John Green
  b. June 15, 1848, New York, N. Y.
  d. Dec, 17, 1918, Sitka, Alaska
  Governor of territory, 1897-99

CLARK, Walter E.
  b. Jan. 7, 1869, Ashford, Conn.
  d. Feb. 4, 1950, Charleston, W. Va.
  Governor of territory, 1909-14

COLE, Thomas
  b. Sept. 17, 1848, Underhill, Vt.
  d. Feb. 3, 1941, Fond du Lac, Wisc.
  Territorial delegate to Congress, 1907-09

DIMOND, Anthony J.
  b. Nov. 30, 1881, Palatine Bridge, N. Y.
  d. May 28, 1953, Anchorage, Alaska
  Territorial delegate to Congress, 1933-45

GRIGSBY, George B.
  b. Dec. 2, 1874, Sioux Falls, Dakota Terr.
  d.
  Territorial delegate to Congress, 1920-21

HOGATT, Wilfred Bacon
  b. Sept. 11, 1865, Paoli, Ind.
  d. Feb. 26, 1938, in Alaska
  Governor of territory, 1906-09

KINKEAD, John M.
  b. Dec. 10, 1826
  d. in Nevada
  Governor of Nevada, 1878-82
  Governor of Alaska territory, 1884-85

KNAPP, Lyman E.
  b. Nov. 5, 1837, Somerset, Vt.
  d. 1904 in Seattle, Wash.
  Governor of territory, 1889-93

RIGGS, Thomas L.
  b. Oct. 17, 1873, Ilchester, Md.
  d. Jan. 16, 1945, Washington, D. C.
  Governor of territory, 1918-21

SHEAKLEY, James
  b. Apr. 24, 1830 in Sheakleyville, Pa.
  d. in Pennsylvania
  Governor of territory, 1893-97

SULZER, Charles A.
  b. Feb. 24, 1879, Roselle, N. J.
  d. Apr. 25, 1919, Sulzer, Alaska
  Territorial delegate to Congress, 1917-19

SUTHERLAND, Daniel A.
  b. Apr. 17, 1869, Cape Breton Is., Can.
  d. Mar. 24, 1955, Abingdon, Pa.
  Territorial delegate to Congress, 1921-31

SWINEFORD, Alfred P.
  b. Sept. 14, 1836, Ashland, Ohio
  d. in Ohio
  Governor of territory, 1885-89

TROY, John W.
  b. Oct. 31, 1868, Dungeness, Wash.
  d. May 2, 1942, Juneau, Alaska
  Governor of territory, 1933-39

WASKEY, Frank H.
  b. Apr. 20, 1875, Lake City, Minn.
  d.
  Territorial delegate to Congress, 1906-07

WICKERSHAM, James
  b. Aug. 24, 1857, Marion County, Ill.
  d. Oct. 24, 1939, Juneau, Alaska
  Territorial delegate to Congress, 1909-17,
    1919, 1921, 1933-35

OUTLINE OF CONSTITUTION

OUTLINE OF CONSTITUTION

Preamble
Article I. Declaration of Rights

Sec. 1. Inherent rights
Sec. 2. Source of government
Sec. 3. Civil rights
Sec. 4. Freedom of religion
Sec. 5. Freedom of speech
Sec. 6. Assembly; petition
Sec. 7. Due process
Sec. 8. Grand jury
Sec. 9. Jeopardy and self-incrimination
Sec. 10. Treason
Sec. 11. Rights of accused
Sec. 12. Excessive punishment
Sec. 13. Habeas corpus
Sec. 14. Searches and seizures
Sec. 15. Prohibited state action
Sec. 16. Civil suits; trial by jury
Sec. 17. Imprisonment for debt
Sec. 18. Eminent domain
Sec. 19. Right to bear arms
Sec. 20. Quartering soldiers
Sec. 21. Construction

Article II. The Legislature

Sec. 1. Legislative power; membership
Sec. 2. Members: qualifications
Sec. 3. Election and terms
Sec. 4. Vacancies
Sec. 5. Disqualifications
Sec. 6. Immunities
Sec. 7. Salary and expenses
Sec. 8. Regular sessions
Sec. 9. Special sessions
Sec. 10. Adjournment
Sec. 11. Interim committees
Sec. 12. Rules

Article IV. The Judiciary

Sec. 1. Judicial power and jurisdiction
Sec. 2. Supreme court
Sec. 3. Superior court
Sec. 4. Qualifications of justices and judges
Sec. 5. Nomination and appointment
Sec. 6. Approval or rejection
Sec. 7. Vacancy
Sec. 8. Judicial council
Sec. 9. Additional duties
Sec. 10. Incapacity of judges
Sec. 11. Retirement
Sec. 12. Impeachment
Sec. 13. Compensation
Sec. 14. Restrictions
Sec. 15. Rule-making power
Sec. 16. Court administration

Article V. Suffrage and Elections

Sec. 1. Qualified voters
Sec. 2. Disqualifications
Sec. 3. Methods of voting; election contests
Sec. 4. Voting precincts; registration
Sec. 5. General elections

Article VI. Legislative Apportionment

Sec. 1. Election districts
Sec. 2. Senate districts
Sec. 3. Reapportionment of house
Sec. 4. Method
Sec. 5. Combining districts
Sec. 6. Redistricting
Sec. 7. Modification of senate districts
Sec. 8. Reapportionment board
Sec. 9. Organization
Sec. 10. Reapportionment plan and proclamation
Sec. 11. Enforcement

Ordinance Number 1. Ratification of Constitution

Ordinance Number 2. Alaska-Tennessee Plan

Ordinance Number 3. Abolition of Fish Traps
Sec. 1. Ballot
Sec. 2. Effect of referendum

SELECTED DOCUMENTS

SELECTED DOCUMENTS

THE FIRST CHARTER OF THE RUSSIAN AMERICAN COMPANY

Issued July 8, 1799 by Czar Paul; published in Petr A. Tikhmenev, *The Historical Review of the Formation of the Russian American Company* (St. Petersburg, 1861; trans. by Dmitri Krenov, Seattle, 1939), Part I, pp. 33-36 supp.

The Russian American Company under patronage of his Imperial Majesty is granted the following privileges for twenty years, beginning from this date:

First. The coast of North-Eastern America discovered of old by Russian navigators, starting from 55 degrees northern latitude and the chain of islands stretching from Kamchatka to the north toward America and to the south toward Japan, being in Russian possession, the Company is granted exclusive rights to trade and to all the establishments now located on the North-Eastern Coast of America from 55 degrees to the Bering Strait and beyond it. Also on the islands--Aleutian, Kurila and others--in the North-Eastern Ocean.

Second. To allow it to make new discoveries not only above 55 degrees of northern latitude but farther south as well, and to occupy the discovered lands in Russian possession as before, provided that they are not occupied by other powers and are not in their possession.

Third. To have exclusive rights to all that has been discovered by the Company in these places, on the surface and below the ground, and to everything that may be discovered in the future. Any claims to these resources by others are to be prohibited.

Fourth. It is permitted to the Company when and where it would be found necessary as a matter of safety to build fortifications and to send ships with goods, supplies and *promishleniki*, without any hindrance.

43

Fifth. To engage in navigation, visiting neighboring peoples and trading with all neighboring Powers, after receiving first their consent and the Emperor's approval, in order to strengthen its establishments and derive profits.

Sixth. To engage men of all classes, free and above suspicion, having valid permits for such employment as navigators, traders and workers for establishments of all kinds. Considering the remoteness of the place for which they are leaving, the (government offices) in Russia are instructed to issue passports to government settlers and to others belonging to free estates for a term of seven years. The peasants belonging to landowners (serfs) and other servants may be hired by the Company only with the permission of the owners. The Company shall pay government taxes for all men employed by the Company.

Seventh. The Sovereign ukase prohibits the cutting of timber without first obtaining a permit from the Admiralty College, but taking into consideration of remoteness of the above-mentioned Board from the Ohotsk province where this Company must make repairs and sometimes construct new ships, it is allowed to use timber without hindrance.

Eighth. It is allowed to sell for cash at cost, for hunting, for signals at sea, and for all emergencies on the mainland of America and on the islands, from 40 to 50 poods of powder from the government warehouse in Irkutsk and up to 200 poods of lead from the factories at Nerchinsk.

Ninth. If a stockholder of the Company becomes indebted to the treasury or to private persons and is unable to pay, his investment in the Company cannot be withdrawn but according to the rules of the Company remains in its possession permanently. According to law, any private property is subject to exaction for non-payment of debt, and the creditor becoming the owner of the shares can have only the dividend until the debt is paid. After the expiration of the term of the charter, the new owner will be in complete possession of this stock.

Tenth. In granting the Company exclusive rights for the term of twenty years, in all the above-described lands and islands, it is prohibited to others to be engaged in trade, acquisitions of any kinds, commerce, discovery of new lands and navigation. The merchants who are engaged in trade, and have their own ships and establishments, in the event that they should not wish to join this Company, may enjoy their enterprises and profits as before, but only until their ships shall return. Thereafter they may not engage in trade independently, under penalty of confiscation of their establishments on behalf of this Company.

Eleventh. The general administration of the Russian American Company is to be recognized by all agencies of the government, as being established for the management of the Company's affairs, and all correspondence and court orders should be addressed to it and not to individual stockholders.

(By his Imperial Majesty:) Be It So.

July 8, 1799
Peterhof.

SECRETARY OF STATE SEWARD'S ADDRESS ON ALASKA

William H. Seward, Secretary of State who had negotiated the purchase of Alaska, visited portions of the new territory in the late summer of 1867. His address at Sitka on August 29, 1869 summarized his impressions of the newest possession of the United States.

Citizens of Alaska, Fellow-citizens of the United States: You have pressed me to meet you in public assembly once before I leave Alaska. It would be sheer affectation to pretend to doubt your sincerity in making this request, and capriciously ungrateful to refuse it, after having received so many and varied hospitalities from all sorts and conditions of men. It is not an easy task, however, to speak in a manner worthy of your consideration, while I am living constantly on shipboard, as you all know, and am occupied intently in searching out whatever is sublime, or beautiful, or peculiar, or useful. On the other hand, it is altogether natural on your part to say, "You have looked upon Alaska: what do you think of it?" Unhappily, I have seen too little of Alaska to answer the question satisfactorily. The entire coast line of the United States, exclusive of Alaska, is 10,000 miles, while the coast line of Alaska alone, including the islands, is 26,000 miles. The portion of the Territory which lies east of the peninsula, including islands, is 120 miles wide. The western portion, including Aleutian Islands expands to a breadth of 2,200 miles. The entire land area, including islands, is 577,390 statute square miles. We should think a foreigner very presumptuous who should presume to give the world an opinion of the whole of the United States of America, after he had merely looked in from his steamer at Plymouth and Boston Harbor, or had run up the Hudson River to the Highlands, or had ascended the Delaware to Trenton, or the James River to Richmond, or the Mississippi no farther than Memphis. My observation thus far has hardly been more comprehensive. I entered the Territory of Alaska at the Portland canal, made my way through the narrow passages of the Prince of Wales Archipelago, thence through Peril and Chatham Straits and Lynn Channel, and up the Chilcat River to the base of Fairweather, from which latter place I have returned through Clarence Straits, to sojourn a few days in your beautiful bay, under the shadows of the Baranoff Hills and Mount Edgecombe. Limited, however, as my opportunities have been, I will, without further apology, give you the impressions I have received.

Of course, I speak first of the skies of Alaska. It seems to be assumed in the case of Alaska that a country which extends through fifty-eight degrees of longitude, and embraces portions as well of the arctic as of the temperate zone, unlike all other regions so situated, has not several climates, but only one. The weather of this one broad climate of Alaska is severely criticised in outside circles for being too wet and too cold. Nevertheless, it must be a fastidious person who complains of climates in which, while the eagle delights to soar, the hummingbird does not disdain to flutter. I shall speak only of the particular climate here which I know.

My visit here happens to fall within the month of August. Not only have the skies been sufficiently bright and serene to give me a perfect view, under the sixtieth parallel, of the total eclipse of the sun, and of the evening star at the time of the sun's obscuration, but I have also enjoyed more clear than there have been cloudy days; and in the early mornings and in the late evenings peculiar to the season I have lost myself in admiration of skies adorned with sapphire and gold as richly as those which are reflected by the Mediterranean. Of all the moonlights in the world, commend me to those which light up the archipelago of the North Pacific Ocean. Fogs have sometimes detained me longer on the Hudson and on Long Island Sound than now on the waters of the North Pacific. In saying this, I do not mean to say that rain and fog are unfrequent here. The Russian pilot, George, whom you all know, expressed my conviction on this matter exactly when he said to me, "Oh, yes, Mr. Seward, we *do* have changeable weather here sometimes, as they do in the other States." I might amend the expression by adding the weather here is only a little more changeable. It must be confessed, at least, that it is an honest climate; for it makes no pretensions to constancy. If, however, you have fewer bright sunrises and glowing sunsets than southern latitudes enjoy, you are favored, on the other hand, with more frequent and more magnificent displays of the aurora and the rainbow. The thermometer tells the whole case when it reports that the summer is colder and the winter is warmer in Alaska than in New York and Washington. It results from the nature of such a climate that the earth prefers to support the fir, the spruce, the pine, the hemlock, and other evergreens rather than deciduous trees, and to furnish grasses and esculent roots rather than the cereals of dryer and hotter climates. I have mingled freely with the multifarious population, - the Tongas, the Stickeens, the Cakes, the Hydahs, the Sitkas, the Kootznoos, and the Chilcats, as well as with the traders, the soldiers, the seamen, and the settlers of various nationalities, English, Swedish, Russian, and American, - and I have seen all around me only persons enjoying robust and exuberant health. Manhood of every race and condition everywhere exhibits activity and energy, while infancy seems exempt from disease, and age relieved from pain.

It is next in order to speak of the rivers and seas of Alaska. The rivers are broad, shallow, and rapid, while the seas are deep, but tranquil. Mr. Sumner, in his elaborate and magnificent oration, although he spake only from historical accounts, has not exaggerated - no man can exaggerate - the marine treasures of the Territory. Besides the whale, which everywhere and at all times is seen enjoying his robust exercise, and the sea-otter, the fur-seal, the hair-seal, and the walrus, found in the waters which embosom the western islands, those waters, as well as the seas of the eastern archipelago, are found teeming with the salmon, cod, and other fishes adapted to the support of human and animal life. Indeed, what I have seen here has almost made me a convert to the theory of some naturalists, that the waters of the globe are filled with stores for the sustenance of animal life surpassing the available productions of the land.

It must be remembered that the coast range of mountains, which begins in Mexico, is continued into the Territory, and invades the seas of Alaska. Hence it is that in the islands and on the mainland, so far as I have explored it, we find ourselves everywhere in the immediate presence of black hills, or foot-hills, as they are variously called, and that these foot-hills are overtopped by ridges of snow-capped mountains. These snow-capped mountains are manifestly of volcanic origin; and they have been subjected, through an indefinite period, to atmospheric abrasion and disintegration. Hence they have assumed all conceivable shapes and forms. In some places they are serrated into sharp, angular peaks, and in other places they appear architecturally arranged, so as to present cloud-capped castles, towers, domes, and minarets. The mountain sides are furrowed with deep and straight ravines, down which the thawing fields of ice and snow are precipitated, generally in the month of May, with such a vehemence as to have produced in every valley immense level plains of intervale land. These plains, as well as the sides of the mountains, almost to the summits, are covered with forests so dense and dark as to be impenetrable, except to wild beasts and savage huntsmen. On the lowest intervale land the cottonwood grows. It seems to be the species of poplar which is known in the Atlantic States as the Balm of Gilead, and which is dwarfed on the Rocky Mountains. Here it takes on such large dimensions that the Indian shapes out of a single trunk even his great war canoe, which safely bears over the deepest waters a phalanx of sixty warriors. These imposing trees always appear to rise out of a jungle of elder, alder, crab-apple, and other fruit-bearing shrubs and bushes. The short and slender birch, which, sparsely scattered, marks the verge of vegetation in Labrador, has not yet been reached by the explorers of Alaska. The birch-tree sometimes appears here upon the riverside, upon the level next above the home of the cottonwood, and is generally found a comely and stately tree. The forests of Alaska, however, consist mainly neither of shrubs, nor of the birch, nor of the cottonwood, but, as I have already intimated, of the pine, the cedar, the cypress, the spruce, the fir, and larch, and the hemlock. These forests begin almost at the water's edge, and they rise with regular gradation to a height of two thousand feet. The trees, nowhere dwarfed or diminutive, attain the highest dimensions in sunny exposures in the deeper canons or gorges of the mountains. The cedar, sometimes called the yellow cedar, and sometimes the fragrant cedar, was long ago imported in China as an ornamental wood; and it not furnishes the majestic beams and pillars with which the richer and more ambitious native chief delights to construct his rude but spacious hall or palatial residence, and upon which he carves in rude symbolical imagery the heraldry of his tribe and achievements of his nation. No beam, or pillar, or spar, or mast, or plank is ever required in either the land or the naval architecture of any civilized state greater in length and width than the trees which can be hewn down on the coasts of the islands and rivers here, and conveyed directly thence by navigation. A few gardens, fields, and meadows have been attempted by natives in some of the settlements, and by soldiers at the military posts, with most encouraging results.

Nor must we forget that the native grasses, ripening late in a humid climate, preserve their nutritive properties, though exposed, while the climate is so mild that cattle and horses require but slight provision of shelter during the winter.

Such is the island and coast portion of Eastern Alaska. Klakautch, the Chilcat, who is known and feared by the Indians throughout the whole Territory, and who is a very intelligent chief, informs me that beyond the mountain range which intervenes between the Chilcat and the Yukon Rivers you descend into a plain unbroken by hills or mountains, very fertile, in a genial climate, and, as far as he could learn, of boundless extent. We have similar information from those who have traversed the interior from the shore of the Portland canal to the upper branches of the Yukon. We have reason, therefore, to believe that beyond the coast range of mountains in Alaska we shall find an extension of the rich and habitable valley lands of Oregon, Washington Territory, and British Columbia.

After what I have already said, I may excuse myself from expatiating on the animal productions of the forest. The elk and the deer are so plenty as to be undervalued for food or skins, by natives as well as strangers. The bear of many families, - black, grizzly, and cinnamon; the mountain sheep, inestimable for his fleece; the wolf, the fox, the beaver, the otter, the mink, the raccoon, the marten, the ermine; the squirrel, - gray, black, brown, and flying, - are among the land fur-bearing animals. The furs thus found here have been the chief element, for more than a hundred years, of the profitable commerce of the Hudson Bay Company, whose mere possessory privileges seem, even at this late day, too costly to find a ready purchaser. This fur-trade, together with the sea fur-trade within the Territory, were the sole basis alike of Russian commerce and empire on this continent. This commerce was so large and important as to induce the governments of Russia and China to build and maintain a town for carrying on its exchanges in Tartary on the border of the two empires. It is well understood that the supply of furs in Alaska has not diminished, while the demand for them in China and elsewhere has immensely increased.

I fear that we must confess to a failure of ice as an element of territorial wealth, at least as far as this immediate region is concerned. I find that the Russian American Company, whose monopoly was abolished by the treaty of acquisition, depended for ice exclusively upon the small lake or natural pond which furnishes the power for your saw-mill in this town, and that this dependence has now failed by reason of the increasing mildness of the winter. The California Ice Company are now trying the small lakes of Kodiac, and certainly I wish them success. I think it is not yet ascertained whether glacier ice is pure and practical for commerce. If it is, the world may be supplied from the glaciers, which, suspended from the region of the clouds, stand forth in the majesty of ever-wasting and ever-renewed translucent mountains upon the banks of the Stickeen and Chilcat Rivers and the shores of Cross Sound.

Alaska has been as yet but imperfectly explored; but enough is known to assure us that it possesses treasures of what are called the baser ores equal to those of any other region of the continent. We have Copper Island and Copper River, so named as the places where the natives, before the period of the Russian discovery, had procured the pure metal from which they fabricated instruments of ore and legendary shields. In regard to iron the question seems to be not where it can be found, but whether there is any place where it does not exist. Mr. Davidson, of the Coast Survey, invited me to go up to him at the station he had taken up the Chilcat River to make his observations of the eclipse, by writing me that he had discovered an iron mountain there. When I came there, I found that, very properly, he had been studying the heavens so busily that he had but cursorily examined the earth under his feet, that it was not a single iron mountain he had discovered, but a range of hills the very dust of which adheres to the magnet, while the range itself, two thousand feet high, extends along the east bank of the river thirty miles. Limestone and marble crop out on the banks of the same river and in many other places. Coal-beds, accessible to navigation, are found at Kootznoo. It is said, however, that the concentrated resin which the mineral contains renders it too inflammable to be safely used by steamers. In any case, it would seem calculated to supply the fuel requisite for the manufacture of iron. What seems to be excellent cannal coal is also found in the Prince of Wales Archipelago. There are also mines at Cook's Inlet. Placer and quartz gold mining is pursued under many social disadvantages upon the Stickeen and elsewhere, with a degree of success which, while it does not warrant us in assigning a superiority in that respect to the Territory, does nevertheless warrant us in regarding gold mining as an established and reliable resource.

It would argue inexcusable insensibility if I should fail to speak of the scenery which, in the course of my voyage, has seemed to pass like a varied and magnificent panorama before me. The exhibition did not, indeed, open within the Territory. It broke upon me first when I had passed Cape Flattery and entered the Straits of Fuca, which separate British Columbia from Washington Territory. It widened as I passed along the shore of Puget Sound, expanded in the waters which divide Vancouver from the continent, and finally spread itself out into a magnificent archipelago, stretching through the entire Gulf of Alaska, and closing under the shade of Mounts Fairweather and St. Elias. Nature has furnished to this majestic picture the only suitable border which could be conceived, by lifting the coast range mountains to an exalted height, and clothing them with eternal snows and crystalline glaciers.

It remains only to speak of man and of society in Alaska. Until the present moment the country has been exclusively inhabited and occupied by some thirty or more Indian tribes. I incline to doubt the popular classification of these tribes upon the assumption that they have descended from diverse races. Climate and other circumstances have indeed produced some differences of manners and customs between the Aleuts, the Koloschians, and the interior continental tribes. But all of them are manifestly of Mongol origin. Although they have preserved no common traditions, all alike indulge in tastes, wear a physiognomy, and are imbued with sentiments peculiarly noticed in Japan and China. Savage communities, no less than civilized nations, require space for subsistence, whether they depend for it upon the land or upon the sea, - in savage communities especially; and increase of population disproportioned to the supplies of the country occupied necessitates subdivision and remote colonization. Oppression and cruelty occur even more frequently among barbarians than among civilized men. Nor are ambition and faction less inherent in the one condition than in the other. From these causes it had happened that the 25,000 Indians in Alaska are found permanently divided into so many insignificant nations. These nations are jealous, ambitious, and violent; could in no case exist long in the same region without mutually affording what, in every case, to each party seems just cause of war. War between savages becomes the private cause of the several families which are afflicted with the loss of their members. Such a war can never be composed until each family which has suffered receives an indemnity in blankets, adjusted according to an imaginary tariff, or, in the failure of such compensation, secures the death of one or more enemies as an atonement for the injury it has sustained. The enemy captured, whether by superior force or strategy, either receives no quarter and submits for himself and his progeny to perpetual slavery. It has thus happened that the Indian tribes of Alaska have never either confederated or formed permanent alliances, and that even at this late day, in the presence of superior power exercised by the United States government, they live in regard to each other in a state of enforced and doubtful truce. It is manifest that, under these circumstances, they must steadily decline in numbers; and, unhappily, this decline is accelerated by their borrowing ruinous vices from the white man. Such as the natives of Alaska are, they are, nevertheless, in a practical sense, the only laborers at present in the Territory. The white man comes amongst them from London, from St. Petersburg, from Boston, from New York, from San Francisco, and from Victoria, not to fish (if we except alone the whale fishery) or to hunt, but simply to buy what fish and what peltries, ice, wood, lumber, and coal the Indians have secured under the superintendence of temporary agents or factors. When we consider how greatly most of the tribes are reduced in numbers and how precarious their vocations are, we shall cease to regard them as indolent or incapable; and, on the contrary, we shall more deeply regret than ever before that a people so gifted by nature, so vigorous and energetic, and withal so docile and gentle in their intercourse with the white man, can neither be preserved as a distinct social community nor incorporated into our society. The Indian tribes will do here as they seem to have done in Washington Territory and British Columbia: they will merely serve their turn until civilized white men come.

You, the citizens of Sitka, are the pioneers, the advanced guard, of the future population of Alaska; and you naturally ask when, from whence, and how soon re-enforcements shall come, and what are the signs and guarantees of their coming? This question, with all its minute and searching interrogations, has been asked by the pioneers of every State and Territory of which the American Union is now composed; and the history of those States and Territories furnishes the complete, conclusive, and satisfactory answer. Emigrants go to every infant State and Territory in obedience to the great natural law that obliges needy men to seek subsistence, and invites adventurous men to seek furtune where it is most easily obtained; and this is always in the new and uncultivated regions. They go from every State and Territory, and from every foreign nation in America, Europe, and Asia, because no established and populous state or nation can guarantee subsistence and fortune to all who demand them among its inhabitants.

The guarantees and signs of their coming to Alaska are found in the resources of the Territory, which I have attempted to describe, and in the condition of society in other parts of the world. Some men seek other climes for health, and some for pleasure. Alaska invites the former class by a climate singularly salubrious, and the latter class by scenery which surpasses in sublimity that of either the Alps, the Apennines, the Alleghanies, or the Rocky Mountains. Emigrants from our own States, from Europe, and from Asia, will not be slow in finding out that fortunes are to be gained by pursuing here the occupations which have so successfully sustained races of untutored men. Civilization and refinement are making more rapid advances in our day than at any former period. The rising States and nations on this continent, the European nations, and even those of Eastern Asia, have exhausted, or are exhausting, their own forests and mines, and are soon to become largely dependent upon those of the Pacific. The entire region of Oregon, Washington Territory, British Columbia, and Alaska, seem thus destined to become a ship yard for the supply of all nations. I do not forget on this occasion that British Columbia belongs within a foreign jurisdiction. That circumstance does not materially affect my calculations. British Columbia, by whomsoever possessed, must be governed in conformity with the interests of her people and of society upon the American continent. If that territory shall be so governed, there will be no ground of complaint anywhere. If it shall be governed so as to conflict with the interests of the inhabitants of that territory and of the United States, we all can easily foresee what will happen in that case. You will ask me, however, for guarantees that the hopes I encourage will not be postponed. I give them.

Within the period of my own recollection, I have seen twenty new States added to the eighteen which before that time constituted the American Union; and I now see, besides Alaska, ten Territories in a forward condition of preparation for entering into the same great political family. I have seen in my own time not only the first electric telegraph, but even the first railroad and the first steamboat invented by man. And even on this present voyage of mine I have fallen in with the first steamboat, still afloat, that thirty-five years ago lighted her fires on the Pacific Ocean. These, citizens of Sitka, are the guarantees, not only that Alaska has a future, but that that future has already begun. I know that you want two things just now, when European monopoly is broken down and United States free trade is being introduced within the Territory: these are military protection while your number is so inferior to that of the Indians around you, and you need also a territorial civil government. Congress has already supplied the first of these wants adequately and effectually. I doubt not that it will supply the other want during the coming winter. It must do this because our political system rejects alike anarchy and executive absolutism. Nor do I doubt that the political society to be constituted here, first as a Territory, and ultimately as a State or many States, will prove a worthy constituency of the Republic. To doubt that it will be intelligent, virtuous, prosperous, and enterprising is to doubt the experience of Scotland, Denmark, Sweden, Holland, and Belgium, and of New England and New York. Nor do I doubt that it will be forever true in its republican instincts and loyal to the American Union, for the inhabitants will be both mountaineers and seafaring men. I am not among those who apprehend infidelity to liberty and the Union in any quarter hereafter; but I am sure that, if constancy and loyalty are to fail anywhere, the failure will not be in the States which approach nearest to the North Pole.

Fellow-citizens, accept once more my thanks, from the heart of my heart, for kindness which can never be forgotten, and suffer me to leave you with a sincere and earnest farewell.

COLONIAL LESSONS OF ALASKA

David Starr Jordan, a widely known commentator of the turn of the century, wrote this article for the November 1898 issue of the *Atlantic Monthly*, decrying the systematic exploitation of the Alaska Territory by various commercial interests.

"And there's never a law of God or man runs north of Fifty-Three."
                                                            Kipling

The United States is about to enter on an experience which the London Speaker cleverly describes as "compulsory imperialism." Wisely or not, willingly or not, we have assumed duties toward alien races which can be honorably discharged only by methods foreign to our past experience. In the interests of humanity, our armies have entered the mismanaged territories of Spain. The interests of humanity demand that they should stay there, and the duties we have hastily assumed cannot be discharged within a single generation.

It is an axiom of democracy that "government must derive its just powers from the consent of the governed." This has been the fundamental tenet of our political system. But government by the people is not necessarily good government. It can never be ideally good until individual intelligence and patriotism rise to a higher level than they have yet reached in any nation whatever. It is possible that government by the people may be intolerably bad. This is the case where individual indifference and greed make effective cooperation impossible. Such a condition exists in several of the so-called republics of the New World, for whose independence our Monroe Doctrine has been solicitous in the past. Such will be the case with the Spanish colonies of to-day, if we leave them to their own devices. For the civic ideas of these people and of their self-constituted leaders rise to no higher plane than those of the vulgar despots from whom they have so long suffered.

In such cases as these, a government, for the time at least, may "derive just powers" otherwise than from the consent of the governed. It may justify itself by being good government. This is, indeed, the justification of the excellent paternal despotism by which "Diaz holds Mexico in the hollow of his hand." It is the foundation of the imperialism of Great Britain. Wherever the flag of England floats it teaches respect for law. There is but one political lesson more important, and that lesson is respect for the individual man. To teach the one has been the mission of England; to teach the other has been the glory of the United States.

The essential function of British imperialism is to carry law and order, "the Pax Britannica," to all parts of the globe. This function has been worked out in three ways, corresponding to England's three classes of tributary districts or colonies. The first class consists of regions settled and civilized by Englishmen already imbued with the spirit of law, and capable of taking care of themselves. In our day such colonies are self-governing, and the bond of imperialism is little more than a treaty of perpetual friendship. Over the local affairs of Canada, for example, England exerts no authority, and claims none. The sovereignty of the home government rests on tradition, and it is maintained through mutual consideration and mutual respect.

A second class of colonies consists of military posts, strategic points of war or of commerce, wrested from some weaker nation at one time or another in the militant past. In the control of these outposts "the consent of the governed" plays no part. The justification of England's rule lies in the use she makes of it. The inhabitants of Gibraltar, for instance, count no more than so many "camp followers." They remain through military sufferance, and the forms of martial law suffice for all the government they need.

The third class of colonies is made up of conquered or bankrupt nations, - people whose own governmental forms were so intolerable that England's paternalism was forced to take them in hand. These countries still govern themselves in one fashion or another, but each act of their rulers is subject to the veto of the British colonial office. "Said England unto Pharaoh, 'I will make a man of you;' " and with Pharaoh, as with other irresponsibles of the tropics, England has in some degree succeeded. But this success has been attained only through the strictest discipline of military methods; not by the method by which we have made a man of Brother Jonathan, not by the means through which republics make free citizens out of the masses of which they are constituted. England has thus become the guardian of the weak nations of the earth, the police force of the unruly, the assignee of the bankrupt. England, as Benjamin Franklin said a century and a half ago, is an island which, "compared to America, is but a stepping-stone in a brook, with scarce enough of it above water to keep one's shoes dry." Yet, by the force of arms, the force of trade, and the force of law, she has become the ruler of the earth. It is English brain and English muscle which hold the world together, and have made it an Anglo-Saxion planet. The final secret of England's strength lies, as I have said, in her respect for law. Good government is the justification of British imperialism. If victories at sea, happy accident, the needs of humanity, "manifest destiny," or any combination of events force foreign dominion on the United States, American imperialism must have the same justification.

It is a common saying of the day that the American flag, wherever once raised, must never be hauled down. This would have the ring of higher patriotism, were another resolve coupled with it: the stars and stripes shall never bring bad government, - shall never wave over misrule, injustice, waste, or neglect. Whatever lands or people may come under our flag, they are entitled to good government, the best that we can give them. This should be better than we give ourselves, for it is not accompanied by the advantages of self-government.

Imperialism can succeed only along lines such as England has already laid down. In the hands of all other nations - except thrifty Holland - the colony has been a source of corruption and decay. It will be so with us, if we follow the prevalent methods of waste and neglect. It is not for the colonies to make us wealthy through taxation and trade. That is the outworn conception which we have forced Spain to abandon. It is for us to enrich them through enterprise and law. There are duties as well as glories inherent in dominion, and the duties are by far the more insistent.

For an object lesson illustrating methods to be avoided in the rule of our future colonies we have not far to seek. Most forms of governmental pathology are exemplified in the history of Alaska. From this history it is my purpose to draw certain lessons which may be useful in our future colonial experience.

Thirty years ago (1867) the United States purchased from Russia the vast territory of Alaska, rich in native resources, furs, fish, lumber, and gold, thinly populated with half-civilized tribes from whose consent no government could "derive just powers" nor any other. In the nature of things, the region as a whole must be incapable of taking care of itself, in the ordinary sense in which states, counties, and cities in the United States look after their own affairs. The town meeting idea on which our democracy is organized could have no application in Alaska, for Alaska is not a region of homes and householders. The widely separated villages and posts have few interests in common. The settlements are scattered along a wild coast, inaccessible one to another; most of the natives are subject to an alien priesthood, the white men knowing "no law of God or man." With these elements, a civic feeling akin to the civic life in the United States can in no way be built up.

It is a common saying among Americans in the north that "they are not in Alaska for their health." They are there for the money to be made, and for that only; caring no more for the country than a fisherman cares for a discarded oyster-shell. Of the few thousand who were employed there before the mining excitement began, probably more than half returned to San Francisco in the winter. Their relation to the territory was and is commercial only, and not civil.

Alaska has an area nearly one fifth as large as the rest of the United States, and a coast line as long as all the rest. Outside the gold fields the permanent white population is practically confined to the coast, and only in two small villages, Juneau and Sitka, can homes in the American sense be said to exist. Even these towns, relatively large and near together, are two days' journey apart, with communication, as a rule, once a week.

When Alaska came into our hands, we found there a native population of about 32,000. Of these, about 12,000 - Thlinkits, Tinnehs, Hydas, etc. - are more or less properly called Indians. Of the rest, about 18,000 - Innuits, or Eskimos, and some 2500 Aleuts - are allied rather to the Mongolian races of Asia. There were about 2000 Russian Creoles and half-breeds living with the Aleuts and Innuits, and in general constituting a ruling class among them, besides a few Americans, mostly traders and miners.

Then, as now, the natives in Alaska were gentle and childlike; some of them with a surface civilization, others living in squalid fashion in filthy sod houses. They all supported themselves mainly by hunting and fishing. Dried salt salmon, or *ukl*, was the chief article of diet, and the luxuries, which as time went on became necessities of civilization, - flour, tea, sugar, and tobacco, - were purchased by the sale of valuable furs, especially those of the sea otter and the blue fox. The Greek Church, in return for its ministrations, received, as a rule, one skin in every nine taken by the hunters. The boats of the natives outside the timbered region of southeastern Alaska were made of the skin of the gray sea lion, which had its rookeries at intervals along the coast. With the advent of Americans the sea lion became rare in southern Alaska, great numbers being wantonly shot because they were "big game;" and the natives in the Aleutian region were forced to secure sea lion skins by barter with the tribes living farther to the north. This process was facilitated by the Alaska Commercial Company, which maintained its trading-posts along the coast, exchanging for furs, walrus tusks, and native baskets the articles needed or craved by the natives.

Of all articles held by the latter for exchange, the fur of the sea otters was by far the most important. Since these animals were abundant throughout the Aleutian region thirty years ago, and the furs were valued at from $300 to $1000 each, their hunters became relatively wealthy, and the little Aleut villages became abodes of comparative comfort. In the settlement of Belkofski, on the peninsula of Alaska, numbering 165 persons all told, I found in the Greek church a communion service of solid gold, and over the altar was a beautiful painting, - small in size, but exquisitely finished, - which had been bought in St. Petersburg for $250. When these articles were purchased, Belkofski was a centre for the sea otter chase. With wise government, this condition of prosperity might have continued indefinitely. But we have allowed the whole herd to be wasted. The people of Belkofski can now secure nothing which the world cares to buy. As they have no means of buying, the company has closed its trading-post, after a year or two of losses and charity. The people have become dependent on the dress and food of civilization. Suffering for want of sugar, flour, tobacco, and tea, which are now necessities, and having no way of securing material for boats, they are abjectly helpless. I was told in 1897 that the people of Wosnessenski Island were starving to death, and that Belkofski, the next to starve, had sent them a relief expedition. I have no information as to conditions in 1898, but certainly starvation is imminent in all the various settlements dependent on the company's store and on the sea otter. Some time ago it was reported that at Port Etches the native population was already huddled together in the single cellar of an abandoned warehouse, and that other villages to the eastward were scarcely better housed. However this may be, starvation is inevitable along the whole line of the southwestern coast. From Prince William's Sound to Attu, a distance of nearly 1800 miles, there is not a village (except Unalaska and Unga) where the people have any sure means of support. "Reconcentrado" between Arctic cold and San Francisco greed, these people, 1165 in number, have no outlook save extermination. For permitting them to face such a doom we have not even the excuse we have had for destroying the Indians. We want neither the land nor the property of the Aleuts. When their tribes shall have disappeared, their islands are likely to remain desolate forever.

The case of the sea otter merits further examination. The animal itself is of the size of a large dog, with long full gray fur, highly valued especially in Russia, where it was once an indispensable part of the uniform of the army officer. The sea otters wander in pairs, or sometimes in herds of from twenty to thirty, spending most of their time in the sea. They are shy and swift, and when their haunts on land are once disturbed they rarely return to them. Any foreign odor - as the smell of man, or of fire, or of smoke - is very distasteful to them. Of late years the sea otters have seldom come on shore anywhere, as the whole coast of Alaska has been made offensive to them. The single young is born in the kelp, and the mother carries it around in her arms like a babe.

In the old days the Indians killed the otters with spears. When one was discovered in the open sea, the canoes closed upon it, and the hunters made wild noises and incantations. To the Indian who actually killed it the prize was awarded; the others, who assisted in "rounding up" the animal, getting nothing. In case of several wounds, the hunter whose spear was nearest the snout was regarded as the killer. This was a device of the priests to lead the Indians to strike for the head, so as not to tear the skin of the body.

Originally, the sea otter hunt was permitted to natives only. By their methods there were never enough taken seriously to check the increase of the species. The Aleut who had obtained one skin was generally satisfied for the year. If he found none after a short hunt, the "sick tum-tum" or "squaw-heart" would lead him to give up the chase.

Next appeared the "squaw-man" as a factor in the sea otter chase. The squaw-man is a white man who marries into a tribe to secure the native's privileges. These squaw-men were more persistent hunters than the natives, and they brought about the general use of rifles instead of spears. A larger quantity of skins was taken under these conditions, but the numbers of sea otters were not appreciably reduced.

The success of squaw-men in this and other enterprises aroused the envy of white men less favorably placed. A law was passed by Congress depriving native tribes of all privileges not shared by white men. This opened the sea otter hunt to all men, and thus forced the commercial companies, against their will, to enter on a general campaign of destruction.

Schooners were now equipped for the sea otter hunt, each one carrying about twenty Indian canoes, either skin canoes or wooden dugouts, with the proper crew. Arrived at the Aleutian sea otter grounds, a schooner would scatter the canoes so as to cover about sixty square miles of sea. It would then come to anchor, and its canoes would patrol the water, thus securing every sea otter within the distance covered. Then a station further on would be taken and the work continued. In this way, in 1895, 1896, and 1897, every foot of probable sea otter ground was examined. At the end of the season of 1897 only a few hundred sea otters were left, most of them about the Sannak Islands, while a small number of wanderers were scattered along remote coasts. Of these, two were taken off Ano Nuevo Island, California, and two were seen at Point Sur. One, caught alive on land, was allowed to escape, its captor not knowing its value. One was taken in 1896 on St. Paul Island, in the Pribilof, and one in 1897 on St. George.

The statistics of the sea otter catch have been carefully compiled by Captain Calvin H. Hooper, commander of the Bering Sea Patrol Fleet, a man to whom the people of Alaska owe a lasting debt of gratitude. These show that in the earliest years of American occupation upwards of 2500 skins were taken annually by canoes going out from the shore, and this without apparent diminution of the herd. Later, with the use of schooners, this number was increased, reaching a maximum of 4152 in 1885. Although the number of schooners continued to increase, the total catch fell off in 1896 to 724, these being divided among more than 40 schooners, with nearly 800 canoes. Very many of the hunters thus obtained no skins at all.

At the earnest solicitation of Captain Hooper, this wanton waste was finally checked in 1898. By an order of the Secretary of the Treasury, Mr. Gage, all sea otter hunting, whether by white men or by natives, was limited to the original Indian methods. In this chase, no one is now allowed "the use of any boat or vessel other than the ordinary two hatch skin-covered bidarka or the open Yakutat canoe."

This simple regulation will prevent any further waste. Had it been adopted two years ago, it would have saved $500,000 a year to the resources of Alaska, besides perhaps the lives of a thousand people, who must now starve unless fed by the government, - a tardy paternalism which is the first step toward extermination. The loss of self-dependence and of self-respect which government support entails is as surely destructive to the race as starvation itself.

Our courts have decided that the Aleuts are American citizens, their former nominal status under Russian law being retained after annexation by the United States. But citizenship can avail nothing unless their means of support is guarded by the government. They have no power to protect themselves. They can have no representatives in Congress. A delegate from Alaska, even if such an official existed, would represent interests wholly different from theirs. They cannot repel encroachments by force of arms, nor indeed have they any clear idea of the causes of their misery, for they have cheerfully taken part in their own undoing. In such case, the only good government possible is an enlightened paternalism. This will be expensive, for otherwise it will be merely farcical. If we are not prepared to give such government to our dependencies, we should cede them to some power that is ready to meet the demands. Nothing can be more demoralizing than the forms of democracy, when actual self-government is impossible.

In general, the waste and confusion in Alaska arise from four sources, - lack of centralization of power and authority, lack of scientific knowledge, lack of personal and public interest, and the use of offices as political patronage.

In the first place, no single person or bureau is responsible for Alaska. The Treasury Department looks after the charting and the patrol of its coasts, the care of its animal life, the prohibition of intoxicating liquors, and the control of the fishing industries. The investigation of its fisheries and marine animals is the duty of the United States Fish Commission. The army has certain ill-defined duties, which have been worked out mainly in a futile and needless relief expedition, with an opera bouffe accompaniment of dehorned reindeer. The legal proceedings within the territory are governed by the statutes of Oregon, unless otherwise ordered. The Department of Justice has a few representatives scattered over the vast territory, whose duty it is to enforce these statutes, chiefly through the farce of jury trials. The land in general is under control of the Department of the Interior. The Bureau of Education has an agent in charge of certain schools, while the President of the United States finds his representative in his appointee, the governor of the territory. The office of governor carries large duties and small powers. There are many interests under the governor's supervision, but he can do little more than to serve as a means of communication between some of them and Washington. It is to be remembered that Alaska is a great domain in itself, and, considering means of transportation, Sitka, the capital, is much further from Attu of Point Barrow than it is from Washington.

The virtual ruler of Alaska is the Secretary of the Treasury. But in his hands, however excellent his intentions, good government is in large degree unattainable for lack of power. Important matters must await the decision of Congress. The wisest plans fail for want of force to carry them out. The right man to go on difficult errands is not at hand, or, if he is, there is no means to send him. In the division of labor which is necessary in great departments of government, the affairs of Alaska, with those of the customs service elsewhere, are assigned to one of the assistant secretaries. Of his duties Alaskan affairs form but a very small part, and this part is often assigned to one of the subordinate clerks. One of the assistant secretaries, Mr. Charles Sumner Hamlin, visited Alaska in 1894, in order to secure a clear idea of his duties. This visit was a matter of great moment to the territory, for the knowledge thus obtained brought wisdom out of confusion, and gave promise of better management in the future.

To this division of responsibility and confusion of authority, with the consequent paralysis of effort, must be added the lack of trustworthy information at Washington. Some most admirable scientific work has been done in Alaska under the auspices of the national government, notably by the United States Coast Survey, the United States Fish Commission, and the United States Revenue Service. But for years a professional lobbyist has posed as the chief authority in Alaskan affairs. Other witnesses have been intent on personal or corporation interests, while still another class has drawn the longbow on general principles. Such testimony has tended to confuse the minds of officials, who have come to regard Alaska chiefly as a departmental bugbear.

Important as the fur seal question has become, its subject matter received no adequate scientific investigation until 1896 and 1897. Vast as are the salmon interests, such investigation on lines broad enough to yield useful results is yet to be made. The sole good work on the sea otter is that of a revenue officer whose time was fully occupied by affairs of a very different kind.

Thus it has come to pass that Alaskan interests have suffered alike from official credulity and official skepticism. Matters of real importance have been shelved, in the fear that in some way or other the great commercial companies would profit by them. At other times the word of these same corporations has been law, when the department might well have asserted its independence. The interest of these corporations is in general that of the government, because they cannot wish to destroy the basis of their own prosperity. To protect them in their rights is to prevent their encroachments. These facts have been often obscured by the attacks of lobbyists and blackmailers. On the other hand, in minor matters the interests of the government and the companies may be in opposition, and this fact has been often obscured by prejudiced testimony.

Another source of difficulty is the lack of interest in distant affairs which have no relation to personal or partisan politics. The most vital legislation in regard to Alaska may fail of passage, because no Congressman concerns himself in it. Alaska has no vote in any convention or election, no delegate to be placated, and can give no assistance in legislative log-rolling. In a large degree, our legislation at Washington is a scramble for the division of public funds among the different congressional districts. In this Alaska has no part. She is not a district filled with eager constituents who clamor for new post-offices, custom-offices, or improved channels and harbors. She is only a colony, or rather a chain of little colonies; and a colony, to Americans as to Spaniards, has been in this case merely a means of revenue, a region to be exploited.

Finally, the demands of the spoils system have often sent unfit men to Alaska. The duties of these officials are delicate and difficult, requiring special knowledge as well as physical endurance. Considerable experience in the north, also, is necessary for success. When positions of this kind are given as rewards for partisan service, the men receiving them feel themselves underpaid. The political "war-horse," who has borne the brunt of the fray in some great convention, feels himself "shelved" if sent to the north to hunt for salmon-traps, or to look after the interests of half-civilized people, most of whom cannot speak a word of English. A few of these men have been utterly unworthy, intemperate and immoral; and occasionally one, in his stay in Alaska, earns that "perfect right to be hung" which John Brown assigned to the "border ruffian." On the other hand, a goodly number of these political appointees, in American fashion, have made the best of circumstances, and by dint of native sense and energy have made good their lack of special training. The extension of the classified civil service has raised the grade of these as of other governmental appointments. The principles of civil service reform are in the highest degree vital in the management of colonies.

As an illustration of official ineffectiveness in Alaska, I may take the control of the salmon rivers by means of a body of "inspectors." In a joint letter to the Assistant Secretary of the Treasury, in 1897, Captain Hooper and I used the following language: -

"At present this work is virtually ineffective for the following reasons: The appointees in general have been men who know little or nothing of the problems involved, which demand expert knowledge of salmon, their kinds and habits, the methods of fishing, and the conditions and peculiarities of Alaska. For effective work, special knowledge is requisite, as well as general intelligence and integrity. These men are largely dependent upon the courtesy of the packing companies for their knowledge of the salmon, for their knowledge of fishing methods, for all transportation and sustenance (except in southeastern Alaska), and for all assistance in enforcing the law. The inspectors cannot go from place to place at need, and so spend much of their time in enforced inaction. They have no authority to remove obstructions or to enforce the law in case of its violation. For this reason, their recommendations largely pass unheeded.

"To remedy these conditions, provision should be made for the appointment only of men of scientific or practical training, thoroughly familiar with fishes or fishery methods, or both, and capable of finding out the truth in any matter requiring investigation. For such purposes, expert service is as necessary as it would be in bank inspection or in any similar specialized work. The department should provide suitable transportation facilities for its inspectors. It should be possible for them to visit at will any of the canneries or salmon rivers under their charge. They should be provided with means to pay for expenses of travel and sustenance, and should receive no financial courtesies from the packing companies, or be dependent upon them for assistance in carrying on their work. The inspectors should be instructed to remove and destroy all obstructions found in the rivers in violation of law. They should have large powers of action and discretion, and they should have at hand such means as is necessary to carry out their purposes."

Under present conditions, the newly appointed inspector, knowing nothing of Alaska, and still less of the salmon industry, is landed at some cannery by a revenue cutter. He becomes the guest of the superintendent of the cannery, who treats him with politeness, and meets his ignorance with ready information. All his movements are dependent upon the courtesy of the canners. He has no boat of his own, no force of assistants, no power to do anything. He cannot walk from place to place in the tall, wet rye-grass, and he cannot even cross the river without a borrowed boat. All his knowledge of the business comes from the superintendent. If he discovers infraction of law, it is because he is allowed to do so, and he receives a valid excuse for it. It is only by the consent of the law-breaker that the infraction can be punished. The law-breaker is usually courteous enough in this regard; for his own interests would be subserved by the general enforcement of reasonable laws. The most frequent violation of law is the building of a dam across the salmon river just above the neutral tide water where the fish gather as if to play, before ascending the stream to spawn. Such a dam, if permanent, prevents any fish from running, and thus shuts off all future increase. Meanwhile, by means of nets, all the waiting fish can be captured. This is forbidden by law, which restricts, the use of nets to the sea beaches. Yet dams exist to-day in almost every salmon river in Alaska; even in those of that most rigidly law-abiding of communities, New Metlakahtla, on Annette Island. The lawlessness of the few forces lawlessness on all.

All that the inspector can do in the name of the government is to order the destruction of an unlawful dam. He has no power to destroy it; and if he had, he must borrow a boat from the company and do it himself. Then, in the evening, as he sits at the dinner table, the guest of the offending superintendent, he can tell the tale of his exploits.

The general relation of the salmon interests to law deserves a moment's notice. Most of the streams of southern and southwestern Alaska are short and broad, coming down from mountain lakes, swollen in summer by melting snows. The common red salmon, which is the most abundant of the five species of Alaska, runs up the streams in thousands to spawn in the lakes in July and August. One of these rivers, the Karluk, on the island of Kadiak, is perhaps the finest salmon stream in the world, having been formerly almost solidly full of salmon in the breeding season. The conditions on Karluk River may serve as fairly typical. A few salmon are smoked or salted, but most of them are put up in one pound tins or cans, as usually seen in commerce. This work of preservation is carried on in large establishments called canneries. One of these factories was early built at Karluk, on a sand-spit at the mouth of the river. All Alaska is government land. The cannery companies are therefore squatters, practically without claim, without rights, and without responsibilities. The seining-ground on the sand-spit of Karluk is doubtless the best fishing-ground in Alaska. The law provided that no fish should be taken on Saturday, that no dams or traps should be used, that no nets should be placed in the river, and no net set within one hundred feet of a net already placed. This last clause is the sole hold that any cannery has on the fishing-ground where it is situated. Soon other factories were opened on the beach at Karluk by other persons, and each newcomer claimed the right to use the seine along the spit. This made it necessary for the first company to run seines day and night, in order to hold the ground, keeping up the work constantly, whether the fish could be used or not. At times many fish so taken have been wasted; at other times the surplus has been shipped across to the cannery of Chignik, on the mainland. Should the nets be withdrawn for an hour, some rival sould secure the fishing-ground, and the first company would be driven off, because they must not approach within a hundred feet of the outermost net. With over-fishery of this sort the product of Karluk River fell away rapidly. Some understanding was necessary. The stronger companies formed a trust, and bought out or "froze out" the lesser ones, and the canneries at Karluk fell into the hands of a single association. All but two of them were closed, that the others might have full work. Under present conditions, Alaska has more than twice as many canneries as can be operated. Some of these were perhaps built only to be sold to competitors, but others have entailed losses both on their owners and on their rivals.

Meanwhile, salmon became scarce in other rivers, and canners at a distance began to cast greedy eyes on Karluk. In 1897 a steamer belonging to another great "trust" invaded Karluk, claiming equal legal right in its fisheries. This claim was resisted by the people in possession, - legally by covering the beach with nets, illegally by threats and interference. More than once the heights above Karluk have been fortified; for to the "north of Fifty-Three" injunctions are laid with the rifle. On the other hand, "Scar-Faced Charley" of Prince William's Sound and his reckless associates stood ready to do battle for their company. In one of the disputes, a small steamer sailed over a net, cast anchor within it, then steamed ahead, dragged the anchor, and tore the net to pieces. In another case, a large steamer anchored within the fishing-grounds. The rival company cast a net around her, and would have wrecked her on the beach. The claim for damages to the propeller from the nets brought this case into the United States courts. Fear of scandal, and consequent injury to the company's interests in the East, is doubtless the chief reason why these collisions do not lead to open warfare. The difficulty in general is not due to the lawlessness of the companies, not to any desire to destroy the industry by which they live. Our government makes it impossible for them to be law-abiding. It grants them no rights and no protection, and exacts of them no duties. In short, it exercises toward them in adequate degree none of the normal functions of government. What should be done is plain enough. The rivers are government property, and should be leased on equitable terms to the canning companies, who should be held to these terms and at the same time protected in their rights. But Congress, which cannot attend to two things at once, is too busy with other affairs to pay attention to this. The utter ruin of the salmon industry in Alaska is therefore a matter of a short time. Fortunately, however, unlike the sea otter, the salmon cannot be exterminated, and a few years of salmon-hatching, or even of mere neglect, will bring it up again.

Of the marine interests of Alaska, the catch of the fur seal is by far the most important, and its details are best known to the public. Whenever the fur seal question promises to lead to international dispute, the public pricks up its ears; but this interest dies away when the blood ceases to "boil" against England. The history of this industry is more creditable to the United States than that of the sea otter and the salmon, but it is not one to be proud of. When the Pribilof Islands came into our possession, in 1867, we found the fur seal industry already admirably managed. A company had leased the right to kill a certain number of superfluous males every year, under conditions which thoroughly protected the herd. This arrangement was continued by us, and is still in operation. If not the best conceivable disposition of the herd, it was the best possible at the time; and to do the best possible is all that good government demands.

We were, however, criminally slow in taking possession of the islands after their purchase from Russia. In 1868, about 250,000 skins of young males (worth perhaps $2,000,000), the property of the government, were openly stolen by enterprising poachers from San Francisco. As only superfluous males were taken, this onslaught caused no injury to the herd. It was simply the conversion to private uses of so much public property, or just plain stealing. After 1868 the Pribilof Islands yielded a regular annual quota of 100,000 skins for twenty years, when "pelagic sealing," or the killing of females at sea, was begun, and rapidly cut down the herd. This suicidal "industry" originated in the United States; but adverse public opinion and adverse statutes finally drove it from our ports, and it was centred at Victoria, where, as this is written, it awaits its *coup de grace* from the Quebec commission of 1898.

During the continuance of this monstrous business, the breeding herd of the Pribilof Islands was reduced from about 650,000 females (in 1868-84) to 130,000 (in 1897). It is not fair to charge the partial extinction of this most important of fur-bearing animals to our bad government of Alaska, inasmuch as it was accomplished by foreign hands against our constant protest. Yet in a large sense this was our own fault, for the lack of exact and unquestioned knowledge has been our most notable weakness in dealing with Great Britain in this matter. The failure to establish as facts the ordinary details of the life of the fur seal caused the loss of our case before the Paris Tribunal of Arbitration. Guesswork, however well intended, was met by the British with impudent assertion. British diplomacy is disdainful of mere opinion, though it has a certain respect for proved fact. Moreover, it was only after a long struggle that our own people were prevented (in 1898) from doing the very things which were the basis of our just complaint against Great Britain.

The other interests of Alaska I need not discuss here in detail. The recent discovery of vast gold fields in this region has brought new problems, which Congress has made little effort to meet. If we may trust the newspapers, our colonial postal system is absurdly inadequate, and the administration of justice remains local or casual. The Klondike adventurers make their own law as they go along, with little responsibility to the central government. Lynch law may be fairly good law in a region whence criminals can escape only to starve or to freeze; but martial law is better, and the best available when the methods of the common law are out of the question.

The real criminals of Alaska have been the "wild-cat" transportation companies which sprang up like mushrooms with the rush for the Klondike. There are three or four well-established companies running steamers to Alaska, well-built, well-manned, and destined to ports which really exist. But besides the legitimate business there has been a great amount of wicked fraud. A very large percentage of the Klondike adventurers know nothing of mining, nothing of Alaska, little of the sea, and little of hardship. These people have been gathered from all parts of the country, and sent through foggy, rock-bound channels and ferocious seas, in vessels unseaworthy and with incompetent pilots, their destination often the foot of some impossible trail leading only to death. I notice in one circular that a graded railroad bed is shown on the map, through the tremendous ice-filled gorges of Copper River, a wild stream of the mountains, in which few have found gold, and from whose awful glaciers few have returned alive. In the height of the Klondike season of 1898, scarcely a day passed without a shipwreck somewhere along the coast, - some vessel foundering on a rock of the Alaskan Archipelago or swamped in the open sea. Doubtless they should have known better than to risk life and equipment in ships and with men so grossly unfit. But the public in civilized lands is accustomed to trust something to government inspection. The common man has not learned how ships may be sent out to be wrecked for the insurance. In established communities good government would have checked this whole experience of fraud; but in this case no one seemed to have power or responsibility, and the affair was allowed to run its own course. The "wild-cat" lines have now mostly failed, for the extent of the Klondike traffic is far less than was expected, and the Alaska promoter plies his trade of obtaining money under false pretenses in some other quarter.

The control of the childlike native tribes of Alaska offers many anomalies. As citizens of the United States, living in American territory, they are entitled to the protection of its laws; yet in most parts of Alaska the natives rarely see an officer of the United States, and know nothing of our courts or procedures. In most villages the people choose their own chief, who has vaguely defined but not extensive authority. A Greek priest is furnished to them by the Established Church of Russia. He is possessed of power in spiritual matters, and such temporal authority as his own character and the turn of events may give him. The post trader, representing the Alaska Commercial Company, often a squaw-man of some superior intelligence, has also large powers of personal influence, which are in general wisely used. The fact that the natives are nearly always in debt to the company tends to accentuate the company's authority. The control of the Greek priest varies with the character of the man. Some of the priests are devoted Christians, whose sole purpose is the good of the flock. To others, the flock exists merely to be shorn for the benefit of the Church or the priest. But there are a few whom to call brutes, if we may believe common report, would be a needless slur on the bear and sea lion.

On the Pribilof Islands, an anomalous joint paternalism under the direction of the United States government and the lessee companies has existed since 1868. The lessees furnish houses, coal, physician, and teacher, besides caring for the widows and orphans. The government agent has oversight and control of all operations on the islands, and is the official superior of the natives, having full power in all matters of government. This arrangement is not ideal, and is in part a result of early accident. It has worked fairly in practice, however, and the natives of these islands are relatively prosperous and intelligent. The chief danger has been in the direction of pampering. With insurance against all accidents of life, there is little incentive to thrift. Outside of the seal-killing season (June and July) the people become insufferably lazy. There are records of occasional abuses of power in the past, - abuses of a kind to be prevented only by the sending of men of honor as agents. In general, self-interest leads the commercial companies to send only sober and decent men to look after their affairs; and the government cannot afford to do less, even for Alaska. Of this the appointing power at Washington seems to have a growing appreciation.

Among the irregular methods of government in Alaska we must mention one of the most remarkable experiments in the civilization of wild tribes yet attempted anywhere in the world. I refer to the work of William Duncan, the pastor and director of a colony of

Simsian Indians at New Metlakahtla. I can only mention Duncan's work in passing, but his methods and results deserve careful study, - far more than they have yet received. The single will of this strong man has, in thirty years, converted a band of cannibals into a sober, law-abiding, industrious community, living in good houses, conducting a large salmon cannery, navigating a steamer built by their own hands, and in general proving competent to take care of themselves in civilized life.

One of the least fortunate acts of the United States Congress in regard to Alaska has been the enactment of a most rigid prohibitory law as to alcoholic liquors. This is an iron-clad statute forbidding the importation, sale, or manufacture of intoxicants of any sort in Alaska. The primary reason for this act is the desire to protect the Indians, Aleuts, and Eskimos from a vice to which they are excessively prone, and which soon ruins them. But a virtuous statute may be the worst kind of law, as was noted long ago by Confucius. This statute has not checked the flow of liquor in Alaska, while it has done more than any other influence to subvert the respect for law. Usually, men who "are not in Alaska for their health" are hard drinkers, and liquor they will have. It is shipped to Alaska as "Florida water," "Jamaica ginger," "bay rum." Demijohns are placed in flour barrels, in sugar barrels, in any package which will contain them. With all this there is a vast amount of outright smuggling, which the Treasury Department tries in vain to check. All southeastern Alaska is one vast harbor, with thousands of densely wooded islands, mostly uninhabited. Cargoes of liquors can be safely hidden almost anywhere, to be removed piece by piece in small boats. Many such cargoes have been seized and destroyed; but the risk of capture merely serves to raise the price of liquor. Once on shore the liquor is safe enough. Upwards of seventy saloons are running openly in Juneau, and perhaps forty in Sitka. There are dives and groggeries wherever a demand exists. Most of the tippling-houses are the lowest of their kind, because, as they are outlaws to begin with, the ordinary restraints of law and order have no effect on them.

In 1878, it is said, a schooner loaded with "Florida water" came to the island of St. Lawrence, in Bering Sea, and the people exhanged all their valuables for drink. The result was that in the winter following the great majority died of drunkenness and starvation, and in certain villages not a person was left. Sometimes the stock in trade of whiskey smugglers is seized by the Treasury officials. But high prices serve as a sort of insurance against capture, and there are ways of securing a tip in advance when raids are likely to occur. This traffic demoralizes all in any way connected with it. But one conviction for illegal sale of liquors has ever been obtained in Alaska, so far as I know; and it was understood that this was a test case for the purpose of determining the constitutionality of the law. A jury trial in any case means an acquittal, for every jury is made up of law-breakers, or of men in sympathy with the law-breaking. This fact vitiates all criminal procedure in Alaska. It should secure the entire abolition of jury trials and other forms of procedure adapted only to a compact civilization.

Whatever laws are made for the control of the liquor traffic in Alaska should be capable of enforcement. They should be supported, if need be, with the full force of the United States. To impose upon a colony laws with which the people have no sympathy, and then to leave these people to punish infraction for themselves, is to invite anarchy and to turn all law into a farce.

Whiskey is the greatest curse of the people of Alaska, - American, Russian, and native. I have not a word to say in favor of its use, yet I am convinced that unrestricted traffic, that any condition of things, would be better than the present law, with its failure in enforcement. The total absence of any law would not make matters much worse than they are. In fact, law would hardly be missed. In any case, Alaska gets along fairly well, - much better than any tropical region would under like conditions. Cold disinfects in more ways than one, and Alaska gets the benefit of it.

We cannot throw blame on the officials at Washington. They do the best they can under the circumstances. The dishonest men at the capital are not many, and most of them the people elect to send there. The minor officials in general are conscientious and painstaking, making the best possible of conditions not of their choosing. The primary difficulty is neglect. We try to throw the burden of self-government on people so situated that self-government is impossible. We impose on them statutes unfitted to their conditions, and then leave to them the enforcement. Above all, what is everybody's business is nobody's, and what happens in Alaska is generally nobody's business. No concentration of power, no adequate legislation, no sufficient appropriation, - on these forms of neglect our failure chiefly rests.

If we have colonies, even one colony, there must be some sort of a colonial bureau, some concentrated power which shall have exact knowledge of its people, its needs, and its resources. The people must be protected, their needs met, and their resources husbanded. This fact is well understood by the authorities of Canada. While practically no government exists in the gold fields of Alaska, Canada has chosen for the Klondike within her borders a competent man, thoroughly familiar with the region and its needs, and has granted him full power of action. The dispatches say that Governor Ogilvie has entire charge through his appointees of the departments of timber, land, justice, royalties, and finances. "The federal government believes that one thoroughly reliable, tried, and trusted representative of British laws and justice, and of Dominion federal power, can better guide the destinies of this new country than a number of petty untried officials with limited powers, and Ogilvie thinks so himself.

Under the present conditions, when the sea otters are destroyed, the fur seal herd exterminated, the native tribes starved to death, the salmon rivers depopulated, the timber cut, and the placer gold fields worked out, Alaska is to be thrown away like a sucked orange. There is no other possible end, if we continue as we have begun. We are "not in Alaska for our health," and when we can no longer exploit it we may as well abandon it.

But it may be argued that it will be a very costly thing to foster all Alaska's widely separated resources, and to give good government to every one of her scattered villages and posts. Furthermore, all this outlay is repaid only by the enrichment of private corporations, which, with the exception of the fur seal lessees, pay no tribute to the government.

Doubtless this is true. Government is a costly thing, and its benefits are unequally distributed. But the cost would be less if we should treat other resources as we have treated the fur seal. To lease the salmon rivers and to protect the lessees in their rights would be to insure a steady and large income to the government, with greater profit to the salmon canneries than comes with the present confusion and industrial war.

But admitting all this, we should count the cost before accepting "colonies." It is too late to do so when they once have been annexed. If we cannot afford to watch them, to care for them, to give them paternal rule when no other is possible, we do wrong to hoist our flag over them. Government by the people is the ideal to be reached in all our possessions, but there are races of men now living under our flag as yet incapable of receiving the town meeting idea. A race of children must be treated as children, a race of brigands, and whatever authority controls either must have behind it the force of arms.

Alaska has made individuals rich, though the government has yet to get its money back. But whether colonies pay or not, it is essential to the integrity of the United States itself that our control over them should not be a source of corruption and waste. It may be that the final loss of her colonies, mismanaged for two centuries, will mark the civil and moral awakening of Spain. Let us hope that the same event will not mark a civil and moral lapse in the nation which receives Spain's bankrupt assets.

SETTLING THE ALASKA-CANADIAN BOUNDARY DISPUTE

For many years the uncertainties of the old Russian-British treaty defining the Alaskan boundary had plagued Canadian-American relations. In the summer of 1903, a joint commission of American, Canadian and British representatives finally effected a settlement, largely favorable to the United States. The news reports from the *New York Times* of October 18, 19, and 21, 1903 reveal the feelings of the times.

The Alaska Boundary Commission to-day reached an agreement whereby all the American contentions are sustained, with the exception of those in relation to the Portland Channel, which Canada wins.

All that now remains to be done is for the Commissioners to affix their signatures to the decision and complete the map which will accompany it. On the map will be marked the boundary line definitely fixing the division of American and British territory, on such a basis that no American citizen will lose a foot of land he already believed he held, while the United States will get all the waterways to the rich Alaskan territory, with the exception of the Portland Channel, which gives Canada the one outlet the Dominion so much needed.

The long-standing dispute was only settled after a week of keen, trying, secret deliberation between the arbitrators. Even up to noon to-day there was an acute possibility that a disagreement might result and the whole proceedings fall to the ground.

Lord Alverstone, though openly inclined to believe in the justice of the American argument that the United States was entitled to the heads of inlets, as contained in Question Five, held out that Canada had established her case in questions Two and Three, dealing with the Portland Channel.

After luncheon Senator Lodge, Secretary Root, and Senator Turner agreed to cede those points and to start the American boundary line from the head of the Portland Channel, thus giving the Canadians that channel and some small islands, on which there are only a few disused storehouses.

This accomplished, the majority of the tribunal agreed to fix, with this exception, the entire boundary as outlined in the American case.

Whether Messrs. Aylesworth and Jette, the Canadian Commissioners, will refuse to sign the decision and make it unanimous, is not yet known. But, it will not affect the validity of the agreement if a minority report is submitted.

By Monday afternoon it is hoped that everything will be ready for signature, though the actual marking of the line on the map which shall forever determine the respective territories will occupy some time.

The majority of the Commissioners left the Foreign Office hurriedly this afternoon in order to catch trains for week-end visits to the country. Nothing had occurred which would lead the few onlookers even to suspect that the dispute had reached its practical end.

When the tribunal adjourned at 3:30 P.M. it was understood that no decision had been reached. Indeed, so general was the impression that none would be reached till next week that several of the counsel and others employed in the case left London soon after the adjournment. However, The Associated Press learned that a vote had been taken and that the decision to grant all the American contentions except that for the Portland Channel, which goes to Canada, had been arrived at.

No hitch occurred during the entire deliberations, and as these progressed, the confidence of the American Commissioners that a decision substantially upholding the American claims would be given increased; but it was admitted that it would be necessary to agree to a compromise on the Portland Channel.

The only really disquieting feature of the situation for the Americans during the last few days had been a vague idea that Chief Justice Alverstone, even if he concluded to take the American view, might be unwilling to go on record with a decision to that effect, and that a disagreement was likely.

DISAPPOINTMENT IN CANADA

The Canadian Government has not yet received any official notification of the proposed decision in the Alaska boundary case. If the decision is as reported, namely, that Portland Canal is to remain in Canadian territory, there is a feeling in official circles that the Dominion has not much for which to give thanks.

Canada, in holding the Portland Canal, retains Wales and Pearse Islands, which overlook Port Simpson, the proposed terminus of the Grand Trunk Pacific. It would be inconvenient to have lost these islands, but they were clearly marked on Vancouver's map as being in Canada.

As the Government has no official information, none of the Ministers will speak upon the subject for publication.

During the discussion of a fast Atlantic steamship service in the House of Commons this afternoon, however, Mr. Gourley, member for Colchester, Nova Scotia, whose speeches in the House have gained for him considerable notoriety, took occasion incidentally to refer to the decision in the Alaska boundary case. He said:

"If the news is correct that we hear in the corridors, and I hope it is not, all that the United States has got to do is to make a claim for Canada and they will get it by boastfulness and dishonest effort. If it is true we might as well throw away our national aspirations. The last two generations of Englishmen were degenerates and cowards. They have had no leader since Pitt died. Thank God Chamberlain is galvanizing them and putting new blood in them."

The Hon. William Ross (Victoria, Cape Breton) protested against speaking about Englishmen in this way, and Mr. Gourley retorted that they went "around with blinders on, unfit to drive sheep across the country."

ALASKA AWARD SIGNED

The engrossed copy of the award of the Alaska Boundary Tribunal was signed shortly after 2 o'clock this afternoon, by Lord Chief Justice Alverstone of the British Commissioners, Secretary of War Root and Senators Lodge and Turner, the American Commissioners.

The Canadian Commissioners, Messrs. Aylesworth and Jette, declined to sign the award, but signed the maps agreed upon by the majority. They will submit their contrary opinions to the tribunal, so as to go officially on record.

In consequence of the attitude maintained by the Canadian Commissioners, Lord Chief Justice Alverstone decided this morning not to hold the proposed public meeting of the Commission, but to hand its decision to Messrs. Foster and Sifton, respective agents of the American and Canadian Governments.

The Canadian Commissioners declared that in case a public meeting was held they would not only decline to sign the award, but would publicly withdraw from the Commission. They as well as all the Canadians connected with the case were very bitter. Telegrams from Premier Laurier and other prominent persons in Canada showed that this sentiment was shared generally throughout the Dominion.

The change in procedure made necessary by the attitude of the Canadians caused much astonishment among the people who crowded the corridors adjoining the waiting rooms. Ambassador Choate as well as the Canadians and others immediately connected with the case were admitted to the room where the tribunal had been holding the open sessions, but the Commissioners remained closeted in the Cabinet room. The Secretary of the commission, Reginald T. Tower, finally emerged and informed the waiting crowd that no public session would be held and that the award would be made public through the agents.

The award relating to Portland Channel gives the United States two islands, Kannaghunut and Sitklan, commanding the entrance of the Portland Channel and the ocean passage to Port Simpson and destroying the strategic value of Wales and Pearse Islands, which are given to Canada.

The mountain line adopted as the boundary line is so far from the coast as to give the United States substantially all the territory in dispute. It completely clears all the bays and inlets and means of access to the sea, giving the United States a complete land barrier between Canada and the sea, from the Portland Channel to Mount St. Elias. Around the head of the Lynn Canal the line follows the watershed, somewhat in accordance with the present provisional boundary.

DIGEST OF THE DECISION

An official digest of the decision of the majority was given out. It is in the form of answers to the seven questions contained in the treaty of 1903. According to this digest the answers were:

Q.-What is intended as the point of commencement of the line?

A.-The line commences at Cape Muzon.

Q.-What channel is the Portland Channel?

A.-The Portland Channel passes north of Pearse and Wales Islands, and enters the ocean through Tongas Passage, between Wales and Sitklan Islands.

Q.-What course should the line take from the point of commencement to the entrance to Portland Channel?

A.-A straight line to the middle of the entrance of Tongas Passage.

Q.-What point on the fifty-sixth parallel is the line to be drawn from the head of the Portland Channel, and what course should it follow between these points?

A.-A straight line between Salmon and Bear Rivers direct to the fifty-sixth parallel of latitude.

Q.-In extending the line of demarcation northward from said point on the parallel of the fifty-sixth degree of north latitude following the crest of the mountains situated parallel to the coast until its intersection with the one hundred and forty-first degree of longitude west of Greenwich subject to the condition that if such line should anywhere exceed the distance of ten marine leagues from the ocean, then the boundary between the British and the Russian territory should be formed by a line parallel to the sinuousities of the coast, and distant therefrom not more than ten marine leagues, was it the intention and meaning of said convention of 1825 that there should remain in the exclusive possession of Russia a continuous fringe or strip of coast on the mainland not exceeding ten marine leagues in width, separating the British possessions from the bays, ports, inlets, havens, and waters of the ocean, and extending from the said point on the fifty-sixth degree of latitude north to a point where such line of demarcation should intersect the one hundred and forty-first degree of longitude west of the meridian of Greenwich?

A.-Answered in the affirmative.

The sixth question was based on the possibility that this question would be answered in the negative, and therefore did not call for a decision.

Q.-What, if any exist, are the mountains referred to as situated parallel to the coast, which mountains, when within ten marine leagues from the coast, are declared to form the eastern boundary?

A.-The majority of the tribunal have selected the line of peaks starting at the head of Portland Channel and running along the high mountains on the outer edge of the mountains, shown on the maps of survey made in 1893, extending to Mount Whipple and thence along what is known as the Hunter line of 1878, crossing the Stikine River about twenty-four miles from its mouth, thence northerly along the high peaks to Kate's Needle, from Kate's Needle to the Devil's Thumb. The tribunal stated that there was not sufficient evidence owing to the absence of a complete survey, to identify the mountains which correspond to those intended by the treaty. This contemplates a further survey of that portion by the two Governments.

From the vicinity of Devil's Thumb the line runs to the continental watershed, thence through White and Taiya, or Chilkoot Passes, westerly to a mountain indicated on the map attached to the treaty as 6,850 feet, thence to another mountain 6,800 feet, and from that point in a somewhat curved line across the head of the glaciers to Mount Fairweather. This places the Canadian outpost on the upper water of Chilkat River in British territory, and the mining camps of Porcupine and Glacier Creek in American territory. From Mount Fairweather the line passes north on high peaks along the mountains indicated on the map by Mounts Pintn, Ruhama, and Vancouver to Mount St. Elias.

LET US END AMERICAN COLONIALISM

The keynote address to the Alaska Constitutional Convention in 1955 was delivered by Governor Ernest Gruening, the scholarly statesman who had led the fight for statehood since World War II. Widely distributed in pamphlet form, the address summarized the years of protest against second-class status under which residents felt they had suffered.

We meet to validate the most basic of American principles, the principle of "government by consent of the governed." We take this historic step because the people of Alaska who elected you, have come to see that their long standing and unceasing protests against the restrictions, discriminations and exclusions to which we are subject have been unheeded by the colonialism that has ruled Alaska for 88 years. The people of Alaska have never ceased to object to these impositions even though they may not have realized that such were part and parcel of their colonial status. Indeed the full realization that Alaska is a colony may not yet have come to many Alaskans, nor may it be even faintly appreciated by those in power who perpetuate our colonial servitude.

Half a century ago, a governor of Alaska, John Green Brady, contemplating the vain efforts of Alaskans for nearly forty years to secure even a modicum of workable self-government, declared:

"We are graduates of the school of patience."

Since that time Alaskans have continued to take post-graduate courses. Today, in 1955, sorely tried through 88 years of step-childhood, and matured to step-adulthood, Alaskans have come to the time when patience has ceased to be a virtue. But our faith in American institutions, our reverence for American traditions, are not only undimmed but intensified by our continuing deprivation of them. Our cause is not merely Alaskans'; it is the cause of all Americans. So we are gathered here, following action by our elected representatives who provided this Constitutional Convention, to do *our* part to "show the world that America practices what it preaches."

These words are not original with me. But they remain as valued and as valid as when they were uttered five years ago. They remain no less valid even if their noble purpose is as yet unfulfilled. We are here to do what lies within our power to hasten their fulfillment.

We meet in a time singularly appropriate. Not that there is ever a greater or lesser timeliness for the application by Americans of American principles. Those principles are as enduring and as eternally timely as the Golden Rule. Indeed democracy is nothing less than the application of the Golden Rule to the Great Society. I mean, of course, democracy of deeds, not of lip-service; democracy that is faithful to its professions; democracy that matches its pledges with its performance. But there is nevertheless, a peculiar timeliness to this Alaskans' enterprise to keep our nation's democracy true to its ideals. For right now that the United States has assumed world leadership, it has shown through the expressions of its leaders its distaste for colonialism. And this antipathy to colonialism - wherever such colonialism may be found - reflects a deep-seated sentiment among Americans.

For our nation was born of revolt against colonialism. Our charters of liberty - the Declaration of Independence and the Constitution - embody America's opposition to colonialism and to colonialism's inevitable abuses. It is therefore natural and proper that American leadership should set its face against the absenteeism, the discriminations and the oppressions of colonialism. It is natural and proper that American leadership should lend such aid and comfort as it may to other peoples striving for self-determination and for that universally applicable tenet of American faith - government by consent of the governed. Indeed, as we shall see, we are pledged to do this by recent treaty commitments.

What more ironical, then, what more paradoxical, than that very very same leadership maintains Alaska as a colony?

What could be more destructive of American purpose in the world? And what could be more helpful to that mission of our nation than to rid America of its last blot of colonialism by admitting our only two incorporated territories - Alaska and Hawaii - to the equality they seek, the equality provided by the long-established and only possible formula, namely statehood?

America does not, alas, practice what it preaches, as long as it retains Alaska in colonial vassalage.

Is there any doubt that Alaska is a colony? Is there any question that in its maintenance of Alaska as a territory against the expressed will of its inhabitants, and subject to the accompanying political and economic disadvantages, the United States has been and is guilty of colonialism?

Lest there be such doubt, lest there be those who would deny this indictment, let the facts be submitted to a candid world.

You will note that this last sentence is borrowed from the immortal document, the Declaration of Independence. It is wholly appropriate to do this. For, in relation to their time, viewed in the light of mankind's progress in the 180 years since the revolt of the thirteen original American colonies, the "abuses and usurpations" - to use again the language of the Declaration - against which we protest today, are as great, if not greater, than those our revolutionary forbears suffered and against which they revolted.

Let us recall the first item of grievance in the Declaration of Independence:

"He has refused assent to laws, the most wholesome and necessary for the public good."

"He," of course, was King George the Third. Put in his place, in place of the "he", his contemporary equivalent, our ruler, the federal government.

Has it, or has it not, "refused assent to laws most wholesome and necessary for the public good?"

We Alaskans know that the answer is emphatically, "Yes, it has."

He, or for the purpose of 1955, *it*, the federal government, has "refused assent," although requested to do so for some forty years, to the following "most wholesome and necessary laws:"

First. A law transferring the control and management of Alaska's greatest natural resource, the fisheries, to the Territory of Alaska, as it transferred the corresponding resources to all other Territories in the past.

Second. It has "refused assent" to a law repealing the thirty-five year old discrimination in the Maritime Law of 1920, the "Jones Act." a discrimination uniquely against Alaska.

Third. It has "refused assent" to a reform of our obsolete and unworkable land laws, which would assist and speed population growth, settlement and development of Alaska. It alone is responsible for over 99% of Alaska being still public domain.

Fourth. It has "refused assent" to a law including Alaska in federal aid highway legislation.

Fifth. It has "refused assent" to a law abolishing the barbarous commitment procedure of Alaska's insane which treats them like criminals and confines them in a distant institution in the states.

Sixth. It has "refused assent" to placing our federal lower court judges, the United States commissioners, on salary, and paying them a living wage.

One could cite other examples of such refusal to assent to "laws most wholesome and necessary for the public good."

But let us instead pass on to the second item for complaint, which is similar to the first, in the Declaration of Independence:

"He has forbidden his Governors to pass laws of immediate and growing importance..."

Substitute for the "He", then the British royal executive, the present American federal executive, and substitute for "his governors", his party leaders in Congress, and recall their vote in the House of Representatives last May 10, killing a law "of immediate and growing importance" - the statehood bill.

Let us go still further down the list of our revolutionary forefathers' expressed grievances, again quoting the Declaration of Independence:

"He has obstructed the administration of Justice, by refusing his assent to laws establishing judiciary powers."

"He", is today the whole federal government. It has for a decade "obstructed the administration of justice" in Alaska by refusing assent to establishing additional judiciary powers, where they were needed, namely in the Third Judicial Division, while repeatedly increasing the number of judges in the "mother country," the 48 states. And although the population of Alaska has more than tripled in the last forty-six years, the number of federal judges established in Alaska in 1909 remains unchanged. And federal judges are the only judges this colony is permitted to have.

Let us look still further in the Declaration of Independence:

"He has affected to render the military independent and superior to the civil power."

Is there much difference between this and the recent presidential declaration that the defense of Alaska, that is to say the rule of the military here, could be better carried out if Alaska remains a Territory?

One could go on at length drawing the deadly parallels which caused our revolutionary forefathers to raise the standard of freedom, although, clearly, some of the other abuses complained of in that distant day no longer exist.

But Alaska is no less a colony than were those thirteen colonies along the Atlantic seaboard in 1775. The colonialism which the United States imposes on us and which we have suffered for 88 years, is no less burdensome, no less unjust, than that against which they poured out their blood and treasure. And while most Alaskans know that full well, we repeat:

"To prove this let the facts be submitted to a candid world."

To begin at the beginning, the Treaty of Cession by which Alaska was annexed, contained a solemn and specific commitment:

"The inhabitants of the ceded territory. . .shall be admitted to the enjoyment of all the rights, advantages and immunities of citizens of the United States. . ."

That was the pledge. The United States has not kept that pledge. Yet a treaty is the highest law of the land. And it is made in the clear view of all mankind.

The United States has broken that pledge for 88 years. It has not admitted the inhabitants of Alaska to the enjoyment of "all the rights, advantages and immunities of citizens of the United States."

"All the rights, advantages and immunities of citizens of the United States" would entitle us to vote for President and Vice-President, to representation in the Congress by two Senators and a Representative with a vote, and would free us from the restrictions imposed by the Organic Act of 1912, and the Act of Congress of July 30, 1886. Obviously we have neither the vote, nor the representation, nor the freedom from restrictions.

We suffer taxation without representation, which is no less "tyranny" in 1955 than it was in 1775. Actually it is much worse in 1955 than in 1775 because the idea that it was "tyranny" was then new. Since the Revolutionaries abolished it for the states a century and three-quarters ago, it has become a national synonym for something repulsive and intolerable.

We are subject to military service for the nation - a privilege and obligation we accept gladly - yet we have not voice in the making and ending of the wars into which our young men are drafted.

In this respect we are worse off than our colonial forefathers. King George III did not impose conscription upon them. They were not drafted to fight for the mother country. Therefore there was no revolutionary slogan "no conscription without representation." But it is a valid slogan for Alaskans today.

The treaty obligation of 1867 is an obligation to grant us the full equality of statehood, for which Alaskans did not press in the first 80 years of their subordination, but which now, overdue, they demand as their right.

But that is only a small part of the evidence of our colonialism under the American flag. Let us submit more facts to a candid world.

First, let us ask, what is a colony? And let us answer that question.

A colony has been defined in a standard college text-book by a Columbia University professor as "a geographic area held for political, strategic and economic advantage."

That, as the facts will show, is precisely what the Territory of Alaska is - "a geographic area held for political, strategic and economic advantage."

The maintenance and exploitation of those political, strategic and economic advantages by the holding power is colonialism.

The United States is that holding power.

Inherent in colonialism is an inferior political status.

Inherent in colonialism is an inferior economic status.

The inferior economic status is a consequence of the inferior political status.

The inferior economic status results from discriminatory laws and practices imposed upon the colonials through the superior political strength of the colonial power in the interest of its own non-colonial citizens.

The economic disadvantages of Alaskans which in consequence of such laws and practices redound to the advantage of others living in the states who prosper at the expense of Alaskans - these are the hall-marks of colonialism.

Let us take a look at these hall-marks of colonialism deeply engraved on the policies of the United States in Alaska in the field of transportation. Transportation is the key to almost all development. None have demonstrated this better than have the Americans within the non-colonial areas of their 48 states where transportation of every kind - railways, highways, airways - have linked, built and developed a dynamic domain of continental dimensions.

First, let us scrutinize sea-borne transportation. It was, for seventy-three years, until 1940, the only form of transportation between Alaska and the states. Alaska suffers a unique discrimination in maritime law.

Thirty-five years ago the Congress passed a merchant marine act which is known officially as the Maritime Act of 1920. In Alaska it is referred to as the "Jones Act," after its sponsor, the late Senator Wesley L. Jones of the state of Washington. The act embodied a substantial modification of existing maritime law. It provided that goods shipped across the United States, destined either for the coastal ports of the Atlantic or Pacific or for shipment across those oceans to Europe or to Asia, could use either American or foreign carriers. The foreign carriers principally involved were Canadian.

For example, a shipper from the Atlantic seaboard or from the industrial cities of the middle west of products destined for points to the west could ship these across the country wholly on American railroads or on Canadian railroads, or partly on either.

And when these goods arrived at their Coast destination, he could send them across the Pacific in either American or foreign vessels, or southward in either. But at that point in the legislation, creating this new beneficial arrangement, two words had been inserted in Article 27 of the Act. Those two words were, "excluding Alaska."

Now what did those two words signify? They signified that Alaska, alone among the nations, or possessions of nations, on earth, was denied the advantages afforded all other areas. The same discrimination, obviously, applies to products shipped *from* Alaska.

What was the purpose of this discrimination? Its purpose was to subject Alaska to steamship service owned in the city of Seattle. Senator Jones no doubt assumed, and correctly that this would be most helpful to some of his constituents there, as indeed it proved to be, but at the expense, the heavy expense, from that time on, of our voteless citizens of Alaska.

This was in 1920. Under the limited self-government which Congress had granted Alaska through the Organic Act of 1912, more limited than had been granted any other territory, Alaska was still a youngster. Nevertheless, the fifth Territorial legislature meeting the next year, 1921, protested strenuously against this specific and flagrant discrimination, and ordered the Territorial Attorney-General to take the matter to court. The Territorial legislators believed, and so expressed themselves, that this new legislation enacted by Congress at the behest of Senator Jones of Seattle, was in violation of the commerce clause of the Constitution, which forbids discrimination against any port of the United States.

The case came to the Supreme Court of the United States on an appeal from a decree of the United States District Court dismissing the suit brought by the Territory and by an Alaskan shipper, the Juneau Hardware Company, which sought to restrain the Collector of Customs in Alaska from confiscating merchandise ordered by the hardware company and others in Alaska from points in the United States shipped over Canadian railroads, through Canadian ports and thence to Alaska by Canadian vessels, or merchandise to be shipped from Alaska to the United States in like manner.

In pleading the cause of the Territory, Alaska's Attorney-General John Rustgard argued that both the Treaty provisions and the specific extension of the Constitution to Alaska by the Organic Act of 1912 rendered the discriminatory clause unconstitutional. It looked like a clear case.

The Government—our government—which was defending this discriminatory maritime Act, was represented by the Solicitor-General of the United States, the Honorable James M. Beck of Pennsylvania.

Let the candid world note well the language of his argument:

"The immunity from discrimination is a reserved right on the part of the constituent states ... The clear distinction of governmental power between states and territories must be constantly borne in mind ... If the fathers had anticipated the control of the United States over the far-distant Philippine Islands, would they, who concern the reserved rights of the states, have considered for a moment a project that any special privilege which the interests of the United States might require for the ports of entry of the several states should be compulsion be extended to the ports of entry of the colonial dependencies...?"

Let the candid world note that the case for the United States was presented on the basis that discrimination against a colonial dependency was proper and legitimate and that "any special privilege" required in the United States would supersede any obligation to a colonial dependency. The colonial dependency involved was and is Alaska.

Mr. Justice McReynolds, in rendering the decision of the court, declared:

"The Act does give preference to the ports of the States over those of the Territories," but, he added, the Court could "find nothing in the Constitution itself or its history which compels the conclusion that it was intended to deprive Congress of the power so to act."

So it was definitely established by the highest court of the land that Congress had discriminated against Alaska, but that, since Alaska was a colonial dependency, such discrimination was permissible and legal.

Every plea by our Alaska legislatures over a period of 35 years to rectify this grave and unjust discrimination has been ignored by successive Congresses. They have "refused assent" to every attempt by Alaska's delegates to secure remedial legislation.

Now the question naturally arises whether this discrimination imposed by the legislative branch of the federal government, approved by the executive branch, and sanctified by the judicial branch, was to prove to be more than a mere statement of the legality of such discrimination. Was it more than a mere affirmation of the subordinate and inferior status of Alaska's colonials as compared with the dominating and superior status of the American citizens of the states? Did this discrimination also carry with it economic disadvantages? Indeed it did.

Several private enterprises in Alaska were immediately put out of business by the action of Congress in 1920 even before the Supreme Court upheld the legality of that Congressional action.

A resident of Juneau had established a mill to process Sitka spruce. He was paying e required fees to the Forest Service and had developed a market for his product in the Middle West where it was used in airplane manufacture. He was shipping it through Vancouver, where it cost him five dollars a thousand to ship by rail to his customers.

The "Jones Act" automatically compelled him to ship his spruce boards by way of Seattle. Here he was charged eleven dollars a thousand, as against the five dollars he had been paying, plus some additional charges, which totalled more than his profit. In consequence his mill was shut down and a promising infant industry, utilizing an abundant but little used Alaskan resource was extinquished. Not only did the "Jones Act" destroy this and other enterprises, but prevented still others from starting and has prevented them ever since. If anyone doubts that political control of the

Territory through remote forces and absentee interests does not cause economic damage to the people of Alaska he need but look at the working of the maritime legislation directed against Alaska and Alaska only.

Its immediate effects were to more than triple the cost of handling Alaska freight in Seattle on purchases made in Seattle, as compared with Seattle-brought cargoes destined for the Orient. Alaska's delegate, at that time, the late Dan Sutherland, testified that the Seattle terminal charges on shipments to Hawaii or Asia were only thirty cents a ton, and all handling charges were absorbed by the steamship lines, the result of competition between Canadian and American railways and steamship lines. But for Alaska, where Congressional legislation had eliminated competition, the Seattle terminal charges on local shipments, that is to say, on goods bought in Seattle distined for Alaska, were one hundred percent higher, or sixty cents a ton wharfage. So Alaskans paid $1.10 a ton for what cost Hawaiians and Asiatics thirty cents a ton—nearly four times as much.

This was by no means all. On shipments anywhere in the United States through Seattle, and destined for points in the Pacific *other* than Alaska, the total handling charges were only thirty cents a ton wharfage, and all other costs were absorbed by railroad and steamship lines. But for identical shipments consigned to Alaska, an unloading charge of sixty-five cents a ton was imposed, plus a wharfage charge of fifty cents a ton, plus a handling charge from wharf to ship of sixty cents a ton. These charges aggregated over five times the cost to a shipper to other points in the Pacific, and had to be paid by the Alaska consignee or shipper, and of course ultimately by the Alaskan consumer.

These damaging figures were presented by Delegate Sutherland at a public congressional committee hearing and made part of the official printed record. No attempt was made by the representatives of the benefitting state-side interests, either then or later, to explain, to justify, to palliate, to challenge, to refute, or to deny his facts.

If there is a clearer and cruder example of colonialism anywhere let it be produced! Here is a clear case where the government of the United States—through its legislative branch which enacted the legislation, the executive branch, through the President, who signed it, and the judicial branch, which through its courts, upheld it - imposed a heavy financial burden on Alaskans exclusively, for the advantage of private business interests in the "mother country."

Nor is even this by any means all on the subject of railroad and steamship discrimination against Alaska, and Alaska alone. In addition to all the above extortions against Alaska's shippers, suppliers and consumers - the direct result of discriminatory legislation - all the railroads of the United States charge a higher rate, sometimes as much as one hundred per cent higher for shipping goods across the continent, if these goods are distined for Alaska.

There is a so-called rail export tariff and a rail import tariff, which apply to a defined geographic area with exceptions made for other areas, which penalizes Alaska and Alaska alone.

Please note that the service rendered by those railroads, for the same distance, is exactly the same, whether the article to be shipped goes ultimately to Alaska or elsewhere in the Pacific or whether it stays on the mainland of the United States. But the charges for Alaska, and Alaska only, on that identical article, for identical mileage, and identical service, are specifically higher, sometimes up to one hundred per cent higher.

This abuse, as well as the others dating from the Jones Act have been the subject of unceasing protest from Alaskans. Alaska's legislatures have repeatedly memorialized the Congress and the federal executive agencies asking for equal treatment. Again and again have Alaska's delegates sought to have the discriminatory clause in the maritime law repealed. But each time the lobbies of the benefitting stateside interests have been successful in preventing any relief action.

How powerful these lobbies are and how successful they have been in maintaining these burdensome manifestations of colonialism may be judged from the unsuccessful efforts of the late Senator Hugh Butler of Nebraska to get the discriminatory words "excluding Alaska" stricken from the Act. He introduced a bill for that purpose.

In a speech on the Senate floor on December 4, 1947, he denounced "the discrimination against the territory in the present law", that is the Maritime Act of 1920, and urged that there was "need for the prompt removal of that discrimination if we are to demonstrate that we are in earnest in our determination to promote the development of Alaska."

In a subsequent communication to Senator Homer Capehart, who was then chairman of a sub-committee on Alaska matters of the Committee on Interstate and Foreign Commerce to which Senator

Butler's bill was referred, Senator Butler specified the character and extent of the abuse which Alaska was suffering, saying:

"To-day after 27 years of operation under the Jones Act of 1920, the carriers have failed to establish satisfactory service.... The Territory is still without adequate transportation to meet its needs.... Most Alaskan coastal towns are not connected with the continental United States, or with each other, by highway or rail. Accordingly they have been at the mercy of a steamship monopoly of long duration. There could be no competition from rail or bus lines which would compel better services or lower rates. American steamship lines have not been able or willing to meet Alaska's transportation requirements. The service has been infrequent and the rates exorbitant."

This caustic language was Senator Butler's. And his testimony and vigorous denunciation are highly significant, not merely because he was very conservative, but because for the first fourteen years of his Senatorial service he was a bitter opponent of statehood for Alaska, a stand which made him the beau ideal of the anti-statehood elements within and without the Territory. He professed conversion to statehood for Alaska in 1954 only a few months before his death. He was still an unqualified opponent of Alaskan statehood when he issued this devastating indictment of the maritime transportation in 1947 and 8.

After going into further detail on the injurious effects on Alaska of the Jones Act, and the fact that most of the "merchandise...food products...and other commodities" shipped to Alaska were "an exclusive Seattle prerogative," Senator Butler continued:

"The passage of this amendment to the Jones Act could well mean the difference between the slow, continued strangulation of Alaska's economy, and the full development of the Territory's vast potentialities."

Senator Butler then spoke of the discriminatory rates in favor of canned salmon, which industry, he pointed out, likewise centered in and around Seattle, saying:

"The people of Alaska have long been subject to higher rates than has the salmon industry, for general cargo. These higher rates are, in fact, a decree penalizing the resident Alaskan for living in Alaska; the lower rates are, in effect, a decree requiring the Alaska resident to make up for whatever deficits accrue from the costs of shipping canned salmon and salmon-cannery needs. ... The strangling

provisions of the present laws would be eliminated by the enactment of S. 1834."

S. 1834 was Senator Butler's bill to remove this manifestation of colonialism.

And Senator Butler concluded:

"The development of Alaska would be accelerated, and justice would be done to those permanent residents of our northwestern frontier, who have, for so many years, struggled valiantly against discouraging circumstances to develop that area."

Despite Senator Butler's powerful position as the Chairman of the Committee on Interior and Insular Affairs when his party controlled the Congress, this legislation failed. It did not even come out of committee. Eight more years have passed since that time; the tragic situation as far as Alaska is concerned, in its key transportation, has further deteriorated. Steamship freight rates have continued to go up and up, far above the levels that Senator Butler termed "exorbitant."

Invariably, whenever the operators announced another rate increase, the Alaska territorial authorities used to request the maritime regulatory agency to secure an audit of the company's books in order to demonstrate that the increases requested were justified. But almost invariably the increases were granted without such audit and often without question. It may well be asked whether, if Alaska were not a colony, but a State, its two Senators might not be reasonably effective in at least securing a demonstration from the carrier that its financial situation justified the rate increase demanded and promptly acceded to by the federal maritime bureau.

But actually, if Alaska were a State, the whole discrimination in the Jones Act would go out of the port-hole. Alaska would then get the same treatment in the transportation of freight that is accorded to every other area under the flag and to foreign countries. But as a colony it gets no consideration in this matter either from the legislative branch, the Congress, or from the executive branch, in this instance the Federal Maritime Board, successor to other agencies similarly subservient to the vested interests within the colonial power.

The net result of those cumulative charges - 50 to 100 per cent higher railroad freight rates to Seattle, higher unloading and transfer charges in Seattle, higher wharfage and higher longshoring charges, and finally higher maritime freight rates to Alaska ports - all higher

than anywhere else for any but Alaskans, has been and is greatly to increase the cost of living in Alaska. This in itself has been and continues to be a great hindrance to settlement and permanent residence in Alaska, a heavy burden on private enterprise in Alaska, a forecloser of new enterprise, and obviously a great obstacle to development.

How absurd in the light of these facts - and others similar to be submitted to our candid world - is the allegation of the small minority of Alaskans and of others "outside" that we are not ready for statehood. How shall we get readier with these handicaps? How can we cope with what conservative Senator Butler described as "the slow, continued strangulation of Alaska's economy," if the throttling grip of colonialism is not loosened?

To complete the maritime picture, beginning last year all passenger travel on American boats has ceased. The Alaska Steamship Line has eliminated it. This is a blow to an infant and potentially great industry in Alaska, the tourist industry, which four years ago the Alaska 1951 legislature sought to develop by establishing the Alaska Visitors' Association, financed jointly by territorially appropriated and publicly subscribed funds.

One postscript remains on the subject of maritime transportation before we pass on to other of Alaska's colonial disadvantages. Though it is invariably pointed out by Congressional opponents of statehood that Alaska is a non-contiguous area, separated from the main body of the 48 states by some 700 miles of foreign territory, or 700 miles of either international or foreign coastal waters, the United States persists in maintaining the coast-wise shipping laws against Alaska. Their removal would make a steamship line eligible for the subsidies which American flag ships in the European, African or Asiatic trade receive. That might, were Congress sufficiently interested, induce some competition in the Alaska steamship trade from other American carriers. That the imposition of the coast-wise shipping laws is not a necessary corollary to being a colony, it proved by the fact that the United States has suspended the coastwise shipping laws for the Virgin Islands. But it has declined to do so for Alaska.

Let us now turn to a third form of transportation: highways. These catchwords of colonialism, "excluding Alaska", likewise apply to our highway transportation. For Alaska is denied inclusion in the Federal Aid Highway Act. From this beneficent legislation enacted in

1916, and repeatedly amended and amplified, Alaska, alone among the States and incorporated territories, is excluded. Even Puerto Rico, which pays no federal taxes whatever, is included. Yet Alaskans pay all taxes, including the federal gas tax.

The Congressionally wrought substitute - annual appropriation - is a witness to colonialism expressed in cold figures. The results are visible in the lack of an adequate Alaskan highway system. After 88 years of colonialism and 40 years after the enactment by Congress of the joint federal aid and state highway program, Alaska has only some 3,500 miles of highway. This is a negligible amount for an area one-fifth as large as the 48 states and with only one railroad.

For the first 38 years after the cession of Alaska no roads were built by any government agency. With Alaska almost totally public domain, highway construction was clearly a federal responsibility. In the next 36 years beginning with the first federal construction in 1905 and the outbreak of World War II, in 1941, the federal government appropriated about nineteen and a half million dollars, an average of a trifle over half a million dollars a year - a pittance. During that same period Alaska contributed some nine million dollars. Thus the federal contribution was 68.4 per cent of the total of twenty-eight and a half million dollars, and Alaska's was 31.6 per cent, a far greater proportion than Alaska with its virtual totality of public domain would have had to pay under the Highway Act, federal funds go for construction and not for maintenance.

After road construction had been transferred from the War Department to the Department of the Interior in 1930, for the next decade or more throughout the nineteen thirties, when the federal government and the States were jointly expanding the national highway network, Alaska was given no new highway construction. Maintenance only was granted. Military requirements brought the Alaska Highway and the Glenn Highway, and in the later 1940's a highway program to satisfy defense needs was begun and carried out for five years. But even that has been brought to a virtual halt. For the past three years the federal program has contained no new highway project. This year a token appropriation was included for the desirable Fairbanks-Nenana road, but at the price of halting construction of the important Copper River Highway. In fact the present greatly reduced program spells little more than slow completion and paving of the military highways begun eight years ago. The federal government seems to be heading us back to mere maintenance.

In contrast the federal aid program in the mother country is being handsomely increased, reaching the largest sums in its history in the current biennial appropriation enacted in the second session of the 83rd Congress.

If Alaska were a State it would be automatically included in the expanding highway program. But as a colony it continues to be discriminated against, and that discrimination, instead of lessening is being aggravated.

By the same token Alaska has been excluded from the administration's one hundred and one billion dollar federal highway program. One of its principal justifications, perhaps the principal justification, for this lavish, yet important and valuable proposal, is that it is in part a civilian defense measure to aid evacuation and dispersal in the event of a shooting war with atomic weapons. Yet the same administration that excludes Alaska from this defense measure wishes to keep Alaska in colonial bondage because of alleged national defense reasons.

The enactment of this multi-billion dollar program was deferred in the last session of Congress because of differences of opinion on how to finance it. But in one respect there was no difference of opinion: Alaska would be taxed for the program even if not included in it. The Eisenhower program, presented by General Lucius Clay, called for long term bonding to be repaid out of general funds, Congressional substitutes, on a more nearly "pay-as-you-go" basis, called for increased taxes on gasoline, tires, and other automobile accessories. Efforts to include Alaska in both programs failed, as did subsequent efforts to exclude Alaska from the tax provisions. So Alaskans will be taxed for benefits accruing solely to the residents of the mother country. What else is this but colonialism, crude, stark, undisguised and unashamed?

When both the presidential and congressional drafts failed of passage, President Eisenhower declared he was "deeply disappointed" and added:

"The nation badly needs good roads. The good of our people, of our economy, and of our defense requires that the construction of these highways be undertaken at once."

As colonials we can merely note that Alaskans are, in the consideration of our President, apparently not part of "our people, our economy and our defense."

There is yet more of humiliating disregard. The federal administration while patently uninterested in developing Alaska through its highways is strongly in favor of completing the Inter-American Highway.

On March 31, last, President Eisenhower in a letter to Vice-President Nixon requested an increase in the current appropriation for the central American portion from five million to seventy-five million dollars, a more than thirteen-fold increase. The President gave several reasons for this massive amplification. Three of them emphasized the important economic contribution to the countries through which this highway passes, and a fourth stressed the security aspects of the road.

We may applaud the purpose to complete the Inter-American Highway, with its economic benefits to Guatemala, Honduras, Salvador, Costa Rica, Nicaragua and Panama. We may even enjoy our participation in this philanthropy to these good neighbors, remembering that it is more blessed to give than to receive, and that every Alaskan is paying his share of that 75 million dollars. Still, some of us may wonder why similar consideration is not vouchsafed to Alaska, whose highway and economic needs are great, whose trade is almost exclusively with the United States, and whose relation to national security is certainly much closer than that of the Central American republics. This wonder in our part would be particularly natural since President Eisenhower seems to exhibit concern about Alaska's defense in connection with statehood.

We have now viewed three flagrant examples of colonialism in three of the major means of transportation, shipping, railways and highways. Let us now look at the fourth - airways.

It is superfluous to signalize our air-mindedness to any group of Alaskans. But the candid world should know that Alaskans fly thirty to forty times more than other Americans, and starting with our bush pilots, early developed a fine system of intra-Alaskan aviation. It was almost wholly an Alaskan enterprise - flown and financed by Alaskans - though for a time without airports, aids to navigation and other assistance provided in the mother country. The Air Commerce Act of 1926 - a sort of federal aid act for aid - did not supply any of these aids to Alaska, although Alaska was included in the legislation. Nevertheless Alaska again suffered the penalty of being a colony, this time at the hands of the federal executive agency entrusted with administration of the Act. This time it was the bureaucrats who "excluded" Alaska. But the Alaskan bush pilots flew anyhow and what we have in the way of airways in Alaska is largely due to their courageous and skillful pioneering.

However, air service between Alaska and the States, which required the approval of federal bureaus and investment of outside capital, lagged far behind. The first commercial service connecting Alaska with the mother country did not take place till 1940, long after American commercial air carriers had spanned the rest of the hemisphere and had established regular service across the Pacific.

Meanwhile the newly created bureaucracies of the Civil Aeronautics Board and the Civil Aeronautics Administration moved into Alaska. They began restricting local enterprise. In the late 1940's, over the widespread protests of Alaskans, the C. A. B. began cracking down on non-scheduled operations, and finally eliminated the "non-scheds" completely. It did not do so in the forty-eight states. Alaska was again the victim of its colonial status. We had no Senators or voting representatives to fend for us.

The successive certification cases which for over a decade have dealt with transportation between the states and Alaska, have been desperate, and not wholly successful, struggles by Alaskans to overcome the inadequate understanding of the Civil Aeronautics Board that air transportation is relatively much more important in Alaska than in the states with their well-established alternative forms of transportation, by railways and highways. Five years ago interior Alaska was saved from insufficient service only by President Trumen's overruling the Board and granting certification to one of the two Alaskan carriers which the Board had denied.

For the last two years our two Alaskan carriers, in the face of steadily mounting traffic, have managed by heroic, all-out effort at least to retain what they had. But it is noteworthy that while the two international carriers serving Alaska, both "mother country" enterprises, have been granted permanent certificates, the certificates for our two Alaskan carriers are only temporary - a handicap to their financing and to their ability to expand.

Alaska's statehood case could rest here. Yet no account of its 88 years would be complete without some notice of the salmon fishery. It comes, this year, pretty close to being an obituary notice.

Here was Alaska's greatest natural resource.

Here was the nation's greatest fishery resource.

For nearly half a century, the federal government has totally ignored, has "refused assent" to the petitions, pleas, prayers, memorials, of legislatures, delegates, governors, and of the whole Alaskan people for measures that would conserve that resource.

The result is written in figures that spell tragedy for Alaska's fishermen and for many others in Alaska's coastal communities whose economy has long depended on the fisheries. The tragedy has deepened year after year. So grave has become the plight that the administration found it necessary to proclaim the fishing villages to be disaster areas. It is a disaster caused by colonialism, and the federal government may charge the costs of disaster relief and loss of federal tax income to its own policies.

From over eight million cases twenty years ago the salmon pack has fallen year by year until in 1955 it has reached the incredible low of 2,382,131 cases, the lowest in 46 years.

Nowhere, as in the Alaska fisheries fiasco, is the lesson clearer or the superiority, in purely material terms, of self-government to colonialism. In neighboring British Columbia and Washington State, where the fisheries are under home rule, and where fish traps have been abolished, the identical resource has not only been conserved but augmented.

It is colonialism that has both disregarded the interest of the Alaskan people and caused the failure of the prescribed federal conservation function. Colonialism has preferred to conserve the power and perquisites of a distant bureaucracy and the control sentee industry. Alaska has been the victim, but the entire nation has also lost heavily.

Let us by way of a footnote make crystal clear how and why this is colonialism - because some defenders of the *status quo* may deny it is, and we don't want the candid world to be confused.

The people of Alaska have repeatedly and unchangingly manifested their overwhelming opposition to fish traps. It isn't necessary to rehearse all their reasons - the results have amply justified the Alaskans' position. But fish trap beneficiaries, residents of the mother country, want to retain their Alaska traps. So the traps are retained. And it is the power and authority of the federal government which retains them. In a clear-cut issue between the few, profiting, non-colonial Americans and the many, seriously damaged, colonial Alaskans, the state-side interest wins hands down. And it wins because the government, which is also supposed to be *our* government, throws its full weight on their side and against us. *That* is colonialism.

It would be impossible in any one address, even one that assumed the length of a Senate filibuster, to list all the wrongs, disadvantages and lack of immunities that Alaska has endured in its 88 years as a territory. They constitute an incredible story. Even for these who know it, it is hard to believe. It is hard for us as Americans who long ago established our faith in American intelligence, competence, good sense, and above all in American fair play, to contemplate the story of American colonialism in Alaska. It has been part of our faith, an abiding faith, that to right deepseated wrongs in America, one but had to make them sufficiently widely known. And our best hope does lie, I am convinced, in making the facts known widely - and especially the overshadowing fact of our colonialism - to our fellow-Americans and to the rest of the candid world. They should know that what progress has been made in Alaska, and it has been substantial and praiseworthy, has been made in spite of these colonial impositions, and largely because of the character and fibre of the colonials themselves. Coming here from the forty-eight states, following the most cherished American trend, the westward march in search of greater freedom and greater opportunity, they brought to the last frontier and to its friendly native population, the very qualities that have made America. Only distantly man-made problems, the problems created by a remote, often unseen officialdom and its beneficiaries in the mother country, have remained unresolved.

Alaskans have striven consistently to resolve them. Let it be recorded that for 43 years, since the first legislature, and before that by individuals and groups, they have pleaded for relief from the abuses a part of which have been detailed.

Yet after two generations not a single one of these please, all of them fair and reasonable, has been granted.

How applicable to Alaska's plight the words of the Declaration of Independence:

"In every stage of these oppressions we have petitioned for redress in the most humble terms. Our repeated petitions have been answered by repeated injury."

Lest these frequent citations from the Declaration of Independence lead anyone to the conclusion that there are any among us who now desire our independence, let such a totally erroneous assumption be promptly corrected. We desire and demand an end to our colonialism. But we seek it through a re-affirmation in deeds for Alaska of the principles which launched the American experiment, and re-application of the practice that has been followed in 35 states.

We Alaskans believe - passionately - that American citizenship is the most precious possession in the world. Hence we want it in full measure; full citizenship instead of half-citizenship; first class instead of second class citizenship. We demand equality with all other Americans, and the liberties, long denied us, that go with it. To adapt Daniel Webster's famous phrase uttered as a peroration against impending separatism, we Alaskans want "liberty *and* union, one and inseparable, now and forever.

But the keepers of Alaska's colonial status should be reminded that the 18th century colonials for long years sought merely to obtain relief from abuses, for which they - like us - vainly pleaded, before finally resolving that only independence would secure for them the "life, liberty and pursuit of happiness," which they felt was their natural right.

We trust that the United States will not by similar blindness to our rights and deafness to our pleas drive Alaskans from patient hope to desperation.

We have been challenged in the course of Congressional debates to show as a pre-requisite that admission of Alaska to statehood would be beneficial to the nation. That test was never applied to earlier territories seeking and securing statehood. But we gladly accept that challenge and willingly subscribe to it as a condition.

The development of Alaska, the fulfillment of its great destiny, cannot be achieved under colonialism. The whole nation will profit by an Alaska that is populous, prosperous, strong, self-reliant - a great northern and western citadel of the American idea. Statehood would automatically bring us far along that high road.

Nothing could more pathetically reveal the lack of understanding regarding Alaska, and the poor advice concerning Alaska that is given and accepted in the highest places, than the presidential pronouncement in the last state-of-the-union message.

"As the complex problems of Alaska are resolved that Territory should expect to achieve statehood."

Bless us! The complex problems of Alaska are inherent in its territorial status; they are derived from its colonial status; they will be largely resolved by statehood and only by statehood.

As was promptly called to President Eisenhower's attention this was like the old story of telling a youngster he must learn to swim before going into the water!

So we return to the proposition that America can scarcely afford to perpetuate its colonialism. Our nation is attempting to lead the world into the pathway of peace. No goal could be more worthy. But to lead effectively, it must not only practice what it preaches. It must carry out its solemn commitments. It can scarcely be critical of nations that break their pledges and break its own. It must first cast the beam out of its own eye before attempting to pull the motes of its neighbors' eyes.

For the United States has pledged its good name and good faith in treaties and agreements far more recent than the Treaty of Cession of 1867. Not that our nation's responsibility for not carrying out those original pledges in regard to Alaska is diminished by the passage of time. But there are recent and even contemporary commitments which demand fulfillment.

Article 73 of the United Nations Charter, dealing with non-selfgoverning territories - and that includes Alaska which must make annual reports to the U.N. - pledges the signatories:

"To the principle that the interests of the inhabitants of these territories is paramount," and further pledges them

"To insure...their political, economic, social, and educational advancement, their just treatment, and their protection against abuses," and, finally, and this is most pertinent, it pledges them

"To develop self-government, to take due account of the political aspirations of the peoples and to assist them in the progressive development of their free political institutions..."

The United States pledged itself to that ten years ago. If the English language has not lost its meaning and the United States its integrity, it should some time ago have, and should now, in any event, "take due account of the political aspirations" of Alaskans and enable them to develop the self-government which they seek.

There is an even more recent commitment - the Pacific charter - signed a year ago, in which the signatory nations, including the United Stated, pledged themselves "to uphold the principle of equal rights and self-determination of peoples," and to re-enforce that principle the signatories further pledged that they were "prepared to continue taking effective practical measures to insure conditions favorable to orderly achievement of the foregoing purposes", namely self-government.

We are agreed that there is only one form of self-government that is possible for Alaska. And so we are drawing up the constitution for the State that we fervently hope will soon come to be. That hope, it is encouraging to note, is shared by the great majority of Americans. If our 88-year experience inevitably leads to strictures of the colonialism that has ruled us, let us remember that it is a course not sanctioned by American public opinion. The Gallup polls, which last recorded an 82 per cent support of Alaskan statehood, the endorsement of virtually every important national organization, demonstrate clearly that the forces in and out of government which would deny Alaska statehood - in fact the government itself - do not represent prevailing American sentiment.

But while we may derive satisfaction and hope there-from, let us not delude ourselves that victory is at hand. It ought to be. But too many solemn pledges to Alaska have been honored in the breach to assure that what ought to be will be.

It may be regrettable - or not - but every generation must fight to preserve its freedom. We have twice in a life-time participated in our nation's fight to preserve them. In Alaska we still have to win them.

This Constitutional Convention is an important mobilization. But the battle still lies ahead, and it will require all our fortitude, audacity, resoluteness - and maybe something more - to achieve victory. When the need for that something more comes, if we have the courage - the guts - to do whatever is necessary, we shall not fail. That the victory will be the nation's as well as Alaska's - and the world's - should deepen our determination to end American colonialism.

SELECTED BIBLIOGRAPHY

Chevigny, Hector, *Russian America* (New York, 1965)

Gruening, Ernest H., *The Battle for Alaska Statehood* (College, Alaska, 1967)

--- *The State of Alaska* (New York, 1954)

Hulley, Clarence C., *Alaska, 1741-1953* (Portland, Ore., 1953)

Okun, S. B. (Carl Ginsburg, trans.), *The Russian American Company* (Cambridge, Mass., 1951)

Sherwood, Morgan, ed., *Alaska and Its History* (Seattle, 1967)

--- *Exploration of Alaska*, 1865-1900 (New Haven, 1965)

Tompkins, Stewart R., *Alaska: Promyshlenik and Sourdough* (College, Alaska, 1945)

NAME INDEX